FOOTBALL TOP 10

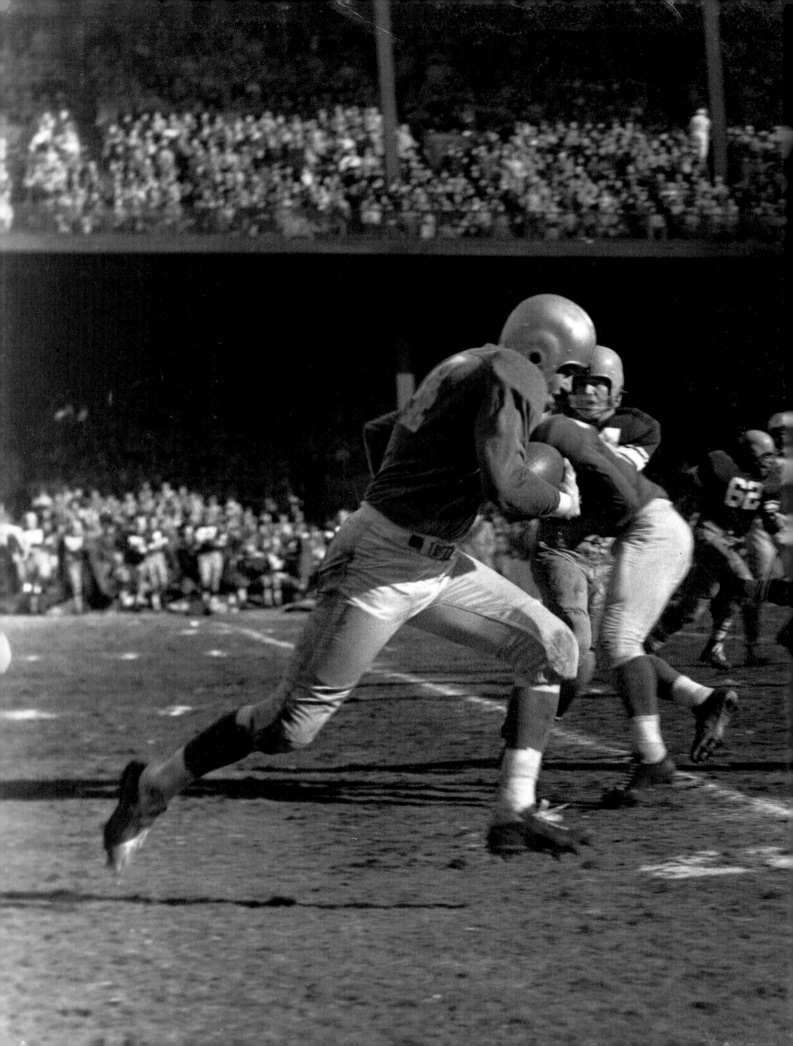

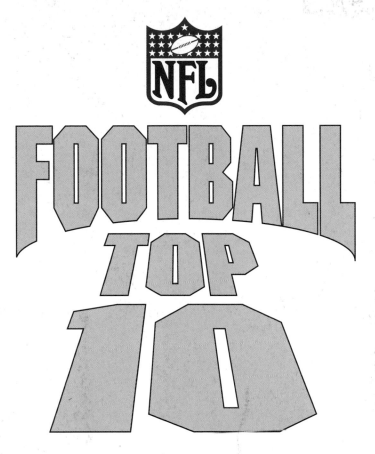

NFL FOOTBALL TOP 10

BY MATT MARINI

CONTENTS

NFL Creative
Vice President/Editor-in-Chief John Wiebusch
Vice President/General Manager Bill Barron
Executive Editor Tom Barnidge
Managing Editor John Fawaz
Executive Art Director Brad Jansen
Football Top 10 **Art Director** Bill Madrid
Assistant Art Director Susan Kaplan
Director-Photo Services Paul Spinelli
Photo Editor Kevin Terrell
Manager-Photo Services Tina Resnick
Director-Manufacturing Dick Falk
Director-Print Services Tina Dahl
Manager-Computer Graphics Sandy Gordon
Publishing Manager Lori Quenneville

LONDON, NEW YORK, MUNICH,
MELBOURNE, AND DELHI

DK Publishing, Inc.
Publisher Chuck Lang
Creative Director Tina Vaughan
Managing Editor Beth Sutinis
Editor Elizabeth Hester
Art Director Megan Clayton
Jackets Art Director Dirk Kaufman

First American Edition, 2002
02 03 04 05 10 9 8 7 6 5 4 3 2 1

Published in the United States by
DK Publishing, Inc.
375 Hudson Street
New York, New York 10014

Copyright © 2002
DK Publishing, Inc.
and NFL Properties LLC

Football top 10. -- 1st American ed.
    p. cm.
    ISBN 0-7894-8841-8 (pbk.)
    1. Football--Records--United States--Juvenile literature.
2. Football--United States--Miscellanea--Juvenile literature. I. Title:
Football top ten. II. Dorling Kindersley Publishing, Inc.

DK Publishing books are available at special discounts for bulk purchases
for sales promotions or premiums. Special editions, including personalized
covers, excerpts of existing guides, and corporate imprints can be created in
large quantities for specific needs. For more information, contact Special
Markets Dept./DK Publishing, Inc./375 Hudson Street/New York, New
York 10014/FAX: 800-600-9098.

see our complete product line at
www.dk.com

Walter Payton

Randall Cunningham

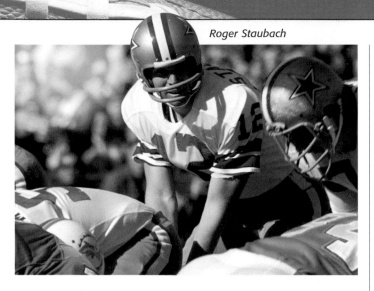

Roger Staubach

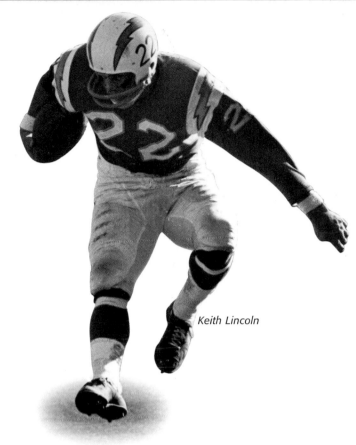

Keith Lincoln

John Taylor

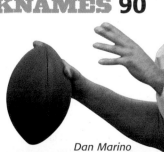

Dan Marino

INTRODUCTION

The first recognized football game took place when the universities of Rutgers and Princeton met on November 6, 1869. The teams used modified London Football Association rules, and the game looked a lot like rugby. In 1876, the first rules for American football were written. The first official professional player was former Yale All-America guard William (Pudge) Heffelfinger, who was paid $500 by the Allegheny Athletic Association in 1892.

Football underwent a dramatic transformation during the next generation. By 1920, the various pro leagues had many problems, including escalating salaries, players jumping teams during the season, and the use of college players. The sport needed an organized league to bring order. So, on August 20, 1920, a dozen men gathered at the Jordan and Hupmobile auto showroom in Canton, Ohio. Their meeting resulted in the formation of the American Professional Football Conference, with all of four teams.

Eight other teams attended the second organizational meeting a month later and renamed the league the American Professional Football Association (APFA). In 1922, the APFA changed its name to the National Football League.

The more than 200 Top 10 lists in this book serve as a tribute not only to the players and coaches who produced the statistics, but also to the scouts who signed them, the high school and college coaches who taught them, and the four clubs that had the foresight to meet in 1920.

COMING INTO ITS OWN
Pro football boomed after World War II, thanks to stars such as Otto Graham (number 60, below), shown leading the Cleveland Browns against the San Francisco 49ers.

TEAM IDENTIFIERS

Many teams have come and gone during the NFL's 82 seasons—35 clubs folded during the 1920s alone—so it can be difficult to keep track of which team did what. The identifiers below are used throughout the book and correspond to the associated teams regardless of changes in nickname or location (e.g. RAM represents Cleveland, Los Angeles, and St. Louis Rams).

ARI	ARIZONA CARDINALS (1994–present)
ATL	ATLANTA FALCONS (1967–present)
BAC	BALTIMORE COLTS (1953–1983, moved to Indianapolis)
BAL	BALTIMORE RAVENS (1996–present)
BOS	BOSTON PATRIOTS (1960–69, moved to New England)
BOY	BOSTON YANKS (1944–48)
BUF	BUFFALO BILLS (1960–present)
CAR	CAROLINA PANTHERS (1995–present)
CHC	CHICAGO CARDINALS (1920–1959, moved to St. Louis)
CHI	CHICAGO BEARS (1921–present)
CIN	CINCINNATI BENGALS (1968–present)
CLE	CLEVELAND BROWNS (1950–1995, 1999–present)
DAL	DALLAS COWBOYS (1960–present)
DAT	DALLAS TEXANS (1960–62, moved to Kansas City)
DEN	DENVER BRONCOS (1960–present)
DET	DETROIT LIONS (1934–present)
GB	GREEN BAY PACKERS (1921–present)
HOU	HOUSTON OILERS (1960–1996, moved to Tennessee)
IND	INDIANAPOLIS COLTS (1984–present)
JAX	JACKSONVILLE JAGUARS (1995–present)
KC	KANSAS CITY CHIEFS (1963–present)
LAC	LOS ANGELES CHARGERS (1960, moved to San Diego)
MIA	MIAMI DOLPHINS (1966–present)
MIN	MINNESOTA VIKINGS (1961–present)
NE	NEW ENGLAND PATRIOTS (1970–present)
NO	NEW ORLEANS SAINTS (1967–present)
NYG	NEW YORK GIANTS (1925–present)
NYJ	NEW YORK JETS (1963–present)
NYT	NEW YORK TITANS (1960–62, renamed New York Jets)
NYY	NEW YORK YANKS (1950–51)
OAK	OAKLAND RAIDERS (1960–1981, 1995–present)
PHI	PHILADELPHIA EAGLES (1933–present)
PHX	PHOENIX CARDINALS (1988–1993, renamed Arizona)
PIT	PITTSBURGH STEELERS (1933–present)
RAI	LOS ANGELES RAIDERS (1982–1994)
RAM	CLEVELAND RAMS (1937–1945), LOS ANGELES RAMS (1946–1994), ST. LOUIS RAMS (1995–present)
SD	SAN DIEGO CHARGERS (1961–present)
SEA	SEATTLE SEAHAWKS (1976–present)
SF	SAN FRANCISCO 49ERS (1950–present)
STC	ST. LOUIS CARDINALS (1960–1987, moved to Phoenix)
TB	TAMPA BAY BUCCANEERS (1976–present)
TEN	TENNESSEE TITANS (1997–present)
WAS	WASHINGTON REDSKINS (1937–present)

DIAMOND JUBILEE
The NFL, which almost failed during the 1920s, celebrated its seventy-fifth anniversary in 1994, an occasion marked by a special patch worn by all players (right, on Steve Young's chest).

TOP 10 PLAYERS

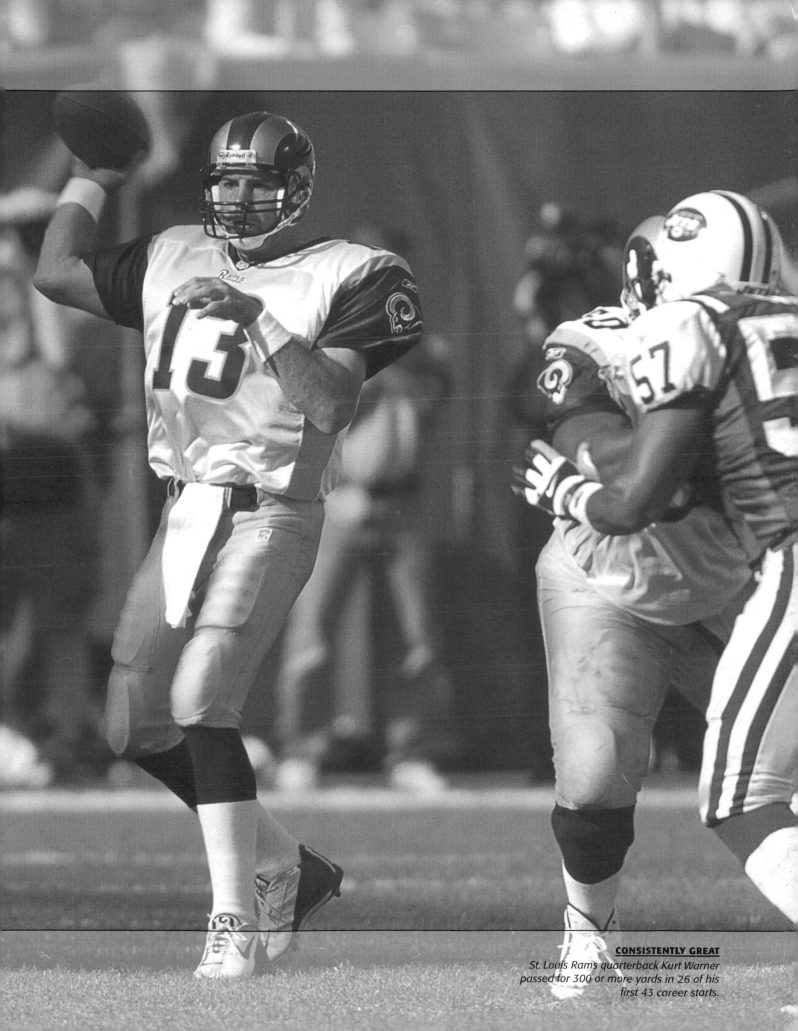

CONSISTENTLY GREAT
St. Louis Rams quarterback Kurt Warner passed for 300 or more yards in 26 of his first 43 career starts.

MOST RUSHING YARDS, CAREER

PLAYER	YARDS
1 Walter Payton	16,726
2 Emmitt Smith*	16,187
3 Barry Sanders	15,269
4 Eric Dickerson	13,259
5 Tony Dorsett	12,739
6 Jim Brown	12,312
7 Marcus Allen	12,243
8 Franco Harris	12,120
9 Thurman Thomas	12,074
10 John Riggins	11,352

Walter Payton broke Jim Brown's rushing record in 1984, and Brown broke the record of Joe (The Jet) Perry in 1963. Perry finished his 16-year Pro Football Hall of Fame career with 9,723 rushing yards, including 1,345 yards he gained in the All-America Football Conference.

UNBREAKABLE?

Jim Brown led the league in rushing yards eight times and in rushing touchdowns five times. Both marks set NFL records that have not been matched.

BREAKING AWAY

Corey Dillon had 7 carries in excess of 20 yards during his record-breaking 278-yard performance against Denver in 2000.

DID YOU KNOW?

Of the 10 rookies who have rushed for 200 yards in a game, only 2—Jim Brown and Tony Dorsett—have been selected to the Pro Football Hall of Fame.

MOST RUSHING YARDS, SEASON

	PLAYER	TEAM	YEAR	YDS
1	Eric Dickerson	RAM	1984	2,105
2	Barry Sanders	DET	1997	2,053
3	Terrell Davis*	DEN	1998	2,008
4	O.J. Simpson	BUF	1973	2,003
5	Earl Campbell	HOU	1980	1,934
6	Barry Sanders	DET	1994	1,883
7	Jim Brown	CLE	1963	1,863
8	Walter Payton	CHI	1977	1,852
9	Jamal Anderson*	ATL	1998	1,846
10	Eric Dickerson	RAM	1986	1,821

In 1934, Beattie Feathers became the first player to rush for more than 1,000 yards in a season—a feat that stood alone for 13 years.

MOST RUSHING YARDS, GAME

	PLAYER	TEAM VS OPP	DATE	ATT	YDS
1	Corey Dillon*	CIN vs. DEN	10/22/00	22	278
2	Walter Payton	CHI vs. MIN	11/20/77	40	275
3	O.J. Simpson	BUF at DET	11/25/76	29	273
4	Shaun Alexander*	SEA vs. OAK	11/11/01	35	266
5	Mike Anderson*	DEN at NO	12/3/00	37	251
6	O.J. Simpson	BUF at NE	9/16/73	29	250
7	Willie Ellison	RAM vs. NO	12/5/71	26	247
8	Corey Dillon*	CIN vs. TEN	12/4/97	39	246
9	Cookie Gilchrist	BUF vs. NYJ	12/8/63	36	243
10	Jim Brown	CLE vs. RAM	11/24/57	31	237
=	Jim Brown	CLE vs. PHI	11/19/61	34	237
=	Emmitt Smith*	DAL at PHI	10/31/93	30	237
=	Barry Sanders	DET vs. TB	11/13/94	26	237

MOST 100-YARD RUSHING GAMES, CAREER

	PLAYER	GAMES
1	Walter Payton	77
2	Barry Sanders	76
3	Emmitt Smith*	74
4	Eric Dickerson	64
5	Jim Brown	58
6	Jerome Bettis*	51
7	Franco Harris	47
8	Thurman Thomas	46
9	Tony Dorsett	45
10	O.J. Simpson	42

Jerome Bettis and O.J. Simpson are the only two players on this list who are not among the NFL's top 10 career rushers. Marcus Allen and John Riggins are ahead of Simpson and Bettis, who rank eleventh and twelfth, respectively, on the all-time rushing list.

NFL NOTEBOOK
Among quarterbacks, Randall Cunningham is the all-time rushing leader with 4,938 yards (through 2001).

MOST 100-YARD RUSHING GAMES, SEASON

	PLAYER	TEAM	YEAR	YARDS	GAMES
1	Barry Sanders	DET	1997	2,053	14
2	Eric Dickerson	RAM	1984	2,105	12
=	Barry Foster	PIT	1992	1,690	12
=	Jamal Anderson*	ATL	1998	1,846	12
5	O.J. Simpson	BUF	1973	2,003	11
=	Earl Campbell	HOU	1979	1,697	11
=	Marcus Allen	RAI	1985	1,759	11
=	Eric Dickerson	RAM	1986	1,821	11
=	Emmitt Smith*	DAL	1995	1,773	11
=	Terrell Davis*	DEN	1998	2,008	11

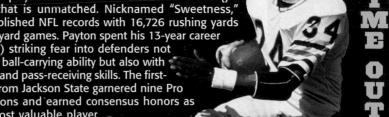

SWEETNESS

Walter Payton played football with a combination of strength and grace that is unmatched. Nicknamed "Sweetness," Payton established NFL records with 16,726 rushing yards and 77 100-yard games. Payton spent his 13-year career (1975–1987) striking fear into defenders not just with his ball-carrying ability but also with his blocking and pass-receiving skills. The first-round pick from Jackson State garnered nine Pro Bowl selections and earned consensus honors as the NFL's most valuable player in 1977.

TIME OUT

RUNNING BACKS

MOST RUSHING TOUCHDOWNS, CAREER

	PLAYER	TDS
1	Emmitt Smith*	148
2	Marcus Allen	123
3	Walter Payton	110
4	Jim Brown	106
5	John Riggins	104
6	Barry Sanders	99
7	Franco Harris	91
8	Eric Dickerson	90
9	Jim Taylor	83
10	Ottis Anderson	81

Emmitt Smith not only has the most career rushing touchdowns, his average of 12.3 scoring runs per season ranks first, too.

BIG DAY
Ernie Nevers (above) rushed for 6 touchdowns and kicked 4 extra points as the Chicago Cardinals defeated the crosstown-rival Bears 40-6 on November 28, 1929.

TOUCHDOWN MACHINE
Emmitt Smith (right) holds the NFL record for rushing touchdowns and holds 3 of the top 10 single-season rushing touchdowns marks.

DID YOU KNOW?
After Jim Brown's retirement, his replacement, Leroy Kelly, proceeded to lead the NFL in rushing touchdowns each of the next three seasons (1966–68).

MOST RUSHING TOUCHDOWNS, SEASON

	PLAYER	TEAM	YEAR	TDS
1	Emmitt Smith*	DAL	1995	25
2	John Riggins	WAS	1983	24
3	Joe Morris	NYG	1984	21
=	Emmitt Smith*	DAL	1994	21
=	Terry Allen*	WAS	1996	21
=	Terrell Davis*	DEN	1998	21
7	Jim Taylor	GB	1962	19
=	Earl Campbell	HOU	1979	19
=	Chuck Munice	SD	1981	19
10	Eric Dickerson	RAM	1983	18
=	George Rogers	WAS	1986	18
=	Emmitt Smith*	DAL	1992	18
=	Marshall Faulk*	RAM	2000	18

MOST RUSHING TOUCHDOWNS, FIRST EIGHT GAMES AS STARTER[#]

	PLAYER	TEAM	YEAR(S)	TDS
1	Eric Dickerson	RAM	1983	12
=	Ickey Woods	CIN	1988	12
3	Shaun Alexander*	SEA	2000–01	10
4	Marcus Allen	RAI	1982	9
=	Joe Cribbs	BUF	1980	9
=	Cleveland Gary	RAM	1990	9
=	Natrone Means	SD	1994	9
=	Billy Sims	DET	1980	9
=	Fred Taylor*	JAX	1998	9
=	Clarence Williams	SD	1979	9

[#]Since 1970

NFL NOTEBOOK
Only four players have rushed for 5 or more touchdowns in a game: Ernie Nevers (6 touchdowns in 1929), Jim Brown (5 in 1959), Cookie Gilchrist (5 in 1963), and James Stewart (5 in 1997).

HIGHEST AVERAGE YARDS PER CARRY, CAREER[#]

	PLAYER	YEARS	ATT	YDS	AVG
1	Randall Cunningham*	1985–2001	775	4,928	6.36
2	Jim Brown	1957–1965	2,359	12,312	5.22
3	Mercury Morris	1969–1976	804	4,133	5.14
4	Gale Sayers	1965–1971	991	4,956	5.00
5	Barry Sanders	1989–1998	3,062	15,269	4.99
6	Napoleon Kaufman	1995–2000	978	4,792	4.90
7	Paul Lowe	1960–1969	1,026	4,995	4.87
8	Lenny Moore	1956–1967	1,069	5,174	4.84
9	Robert Smith	1993–2000	1,411	6,818	4.83
10	Joe Perry	1950–1963	1,737	8,378	4.82

[#]Minimum 750 attempts

HIGHEST AVERAGE YARDS PER CARRY, SEASON

	PLAYER	TEAM	YEAR	ATT	YDS	AVG
1	Beattie Feathers	CHI	1934	119	1,004	8.44
2	Randall Cunningham*	PHI	1990	118	942	7.98
3	Bobby Douglass	CHI	1972	141	968	6.87
4	Dan Towler	RAM	1951	126	854	6.78
5	Steve McNair*	TEN	1997	101	674	6.67
6	Keith Lincoln	SD	1963	128	826	6.45
7	Mercury Morris	MIA	1973	149	954	6.40
8	Jim Brown	CLE	1963	291	1,863	6.40
9	Paul Lowe	LAC	1960	136	855	6.29
10	Dutch Clark	DET	1934	123	763	6.20

TIME OUT

FAST START
The Los Angeles Rams selected Eric Dickerson with the second pick of the 1983 NFL Draft, and the former SMU running back did not disappoint his new team. Dickerson established still-standing NFL rookie records for rushing yards (1,808) and rushing touchdowns (18). In his second season, Dickerson's 2,105 rushing yards set a league record. He also led the NFL in rushing in 1986 and 1988, before finishing his career with the Falcons in 1993.

* Active through 2001 season

MOST RUSHING YARDS, ROOKIE SEASON

	PLAYER	TEAM	YEAR	YDS
1	Eric Dickerson	RAM	1983	1,808
2	George Rogers	NO	1981	1,674
3	Ottis Anderson	STC	1979	1,605
4	Edgerrin James*	IND	1999	1,553
5	Curtis Martin*	NE	1995	1,487
=	Mike Anderson*	DEN	2000	1,487
7	Barry Sanders	DET	1989	1,470
8	Earl Campbell	HOU	1978	1,450
9	Curt Warner	SEA	1983	1,449
10	Jerome Bettis*	RAM	1993	1,429

MOST RUSHING ATTEMPTS, ROOKIE SEASON

	PLAYER	TEAM	YEAR	ATT
1	Eric Dickerson	RAM	1983	390
2	George Rogers	NO	1981	378
3	Edgerrin James*	IND	1999	369
4	Curtis Martin*	NE	1995	368
5	LaDainian Tomlinson*	SD	2001	339
6	Curt Warner	SEA	1983	335
=	Eddie George*	HOU	1996	335
8	Ottis Anderson	STC	1979	331
9	Marshall Faulk*	IND	1994	314
10	Billy Sims	DET	1980	313

MOST RUSHING ATTEMPTS, CAREER

	PLAYER	ATT
1	Walter Payton	3,838
2	Emmitt Smith*	3,798
3	Barry Sanders	3,062
4	Marcus Allen	3,022
5	Eric Dickerson	2,996
6	Franco Harris	2,949
7	Tony Dorsett	2,936
8	John Riggins	2,916
9	Thurman Thomas	2,877
10	Jerome Bettis*	2,686

MOST 100-YARD RUSHING GAMES, ROOKIE SEASON

	PLAYER	TEAM	YEAR	YARDS	GMS
1	Edgerrin James*	IND	1999	1,553	10
2	Ottis Anderson	STC	1979	1,605	9
=	George Rogers	NO	1981	1,674	9
=	Eric Dickerson	RAM	1983	1,808	9
=	Curtis Martin*	NE	1995	1,487	9
6	Franco Harris	PIT	1972	1,055	7
=	Don Woods	SD	1974	1,162	7
=	Earl Campbell	HOU	1978	1,450	7
=	Barry Sanders	DET	1989	1,470	7
=	Jerome Bettis*	RAM	1993	1,429	7

MOST RUSHING ATTEMPTS, SEASON

	PLAYER	TEAM	YEAR	ATT
1	Jamal Anderson*	ATL	1998	410
2	James Wilder	TB	1984	407
3	Eric Dickerson	RAM	1986	404
4	Eddie George*	TEN	2000	403
5	Gerald Riggs	ATL	1985	397
6	Terrell Davis*	DEN	1998	392
7	Eric Dickerson	RAM	1983	390
=	Barry Foster	PIT	1992	390
9	Eric Dickerson	IND	1988	388
10	Edgerrin James*	IND	2000	387

THE RIGHT CHOICE

When the Indianapolis Colts traded Marshall Faulk to the St. Louis Rams two days before the 1999 NFL Draft, many people thought the Colts were going to select University of Texas running back Ricky Williams, the 1998 Heisman Trophy winner, with the fourth pick. Instead, the Colts drafted Edgerrin James out of the University of Miami. James immediately meshed with Peyton Manning, Marvin Harrison, and the rest of the Colts' offense, as he became the eighth player in NFL history to post consecutive 100-yard rushing games at the start of his career. James set an NFL rookie record with ten 100-yard rushing games, joined Eric Dickerson as the only rookies in NFL history with 2,000 yards from scrimmage, and his 17 touchdowns have only been surpassed by Pro Football Hall of Fame members Gale Sayers and Dickerson. It looks like the Colts made the right choice.

TIME OUT

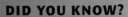
DID YOU KNOW?
In 1988, seldom-used rookie Jamie Morris of the Washington Redskins set an NFL record with 45 rushing attempts (gaining 152 yards) in the season finale, an overtime loss to the Bengals.

MOST SEASONS WITH 1,000 RUSHING YARDS

PLAYER	YEARS
1 Emmitt Smith*	11
2 Walter Payton	10
= Barry Sanders	10
4 Franco Harris	8
= Tony Dorsett	8
= Thurman Thomas	8
= Jerome Bettis*	8
8 Jim Brown	7
= Eric Dickerson	7
= Ricky Watters*	7
= Curtis Martin*	7
= Marshall Faulk*	7

WORKHORSE
The Atlanta Falcons rode Jamal Anderson to an NFL-record 410 carries in 1998 en route to a 14-2 record and a trip to Super Bowl XXXIII.

DANCING BARRY
Barry Sanders dazzled opponents, teammates, and fans alike with his magical moves, prompting Hall of Fame runner Gale Sayers to say, "He's the only back I'd pay to see play."

* Active through 2001 season

QUARTERBACKS

MOST PASSING YARDS, CAREER

	PLAYER	YARDS
1	Dan Marino	61,361
2	John Elway	51,475
3	Warren Moon	49,325
4	Fran Tarkenton	47,003
5	Dan Fouts	43,040
6	Joe Montana	40,551
7	Johnny Unitas	40,239
8	Vinny Testaverde*	39,059
9	Brett Favre*	38,627
10	Dave Krieg	38,147

MOST PASSING YARDS, SEASON

	PLAYER	TEAM	YEAR	YDS
1	Dan Marino	MIA	1984	5,084
2	Kurt Warner*	RAM	2001	4,830
3	Dan Fouts	SD	1981	4,802
4	Dan Marino	MIA	1986	4,746
5	Dan Fouts	SD	1980	4,715
6	Warren Moon	HOU	1991	4,690
7	Warren Moon	HOU	1990	4,689
8	Neil Lomax	STC	1984	4,614
9	Drew Bledsoe*	NE	1994	4,555
10	Lynn Dickey	GB	1983	4,458

AIR CORYELL

Behind the prolific arm of Dan Fouts, the Chargers led the NFL in offense four consecutive seasons (1980–83), averaging 27 points per game during that span.

NFL NOTEBOOK

Only three quarterbacks have posted consecutive 400-yard passing games: Dan Fouts (Chargers, 1982), Dan Marino (Dolphins, 1984), and Phil Simms (Giants, 1985).

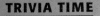

TRIVIA TIME

Dan Marino is one of only two players who have led the NFL in passing yards five times. Can you name the other quarterback to do so?

A: Sonny Jurgensen

AIRING IT OUT

Norm Van Brocklin's 554 passing yards for the high-flying 1951 Rams established a mark that has yet to be surpassed in half a century.

MOST 300-YARD PASSING GAMES, SEASON

	PLAYER	TEAM	YEAR	GMS
1	Dan Marino	MIA	1984	9
=	Warren Moon	HOU	1990	9
=	Kurt Warner*	RAM	1999	9
=	Kurt Warner*	RAM	2001	9
5	Dan Fouts	SD	1980	8
=	Kurt Warner*	RAM	2000	8
7	Dan Fouts	SD	1981	7
=	Bill Kenney	KC	1983	7
=	Neil Lomax	STC	1984	7
=	Dan Fouts	SD	1985	7
=	Brett Favre*	GB	1995	7
=	Steve Young	SF	1998	7

MOST CONSECUTIVE 300-YARD PASSING GAMES

	PLAYER	TEAM	YEAR(S)	GMS
1	Steve Young	SF	1998	6
=	Kurt Warner*	RAM	2000	6
3	Joe Montana	SF	1982	5
4	Dan Fouts	SD	1979	4
=	Dan Fouts	SD	1980–81	4
=	Bill Kenney	KC	1983	4
=	Joe Montana	SF	1985–86	4
=	Joe Montana	SF	1990	4
=	Warren Moon	HOU	1990	4
=	Drew Bledsoe*	NE	1993–94	4
=	Kurt Warner*	RAM	1999	4

MOST 400-YARD PASSING GAMES, CAREER

	PLAYER	GAMES
1	Dan Marino	13
2	Joe Montana	7
=	Warren Moon	7
4	Dan Fouts	6
5	Sonny Jurgensen	5
=	Dave Krieg	5
7	Drew Bledsoe*	4
=	Boomer Esiason	4
=	Tommy Kramer	4
=	Vinny Testaverde*	4

MOST PASSING YARDS, GAME

	PLAYER	TEAM VS OPP	DATE	YDS
1	Norm Van Brocklin	RAM vs. NYY	9/28/51	554
2	Warren Moon	HOU at KC	12/16/90	527
3	Boomer Esiason	ARI at WAS	11/10/96	522
4	Dan Marino	MIA vs. NYJ	10/23/88	521
5	Phil Simms	NYG at CIN	10/13/85	513
6	Vince Ferragamo	RAM vs. CHI	12/26/82	509
7	Y.A. Tittle	NYG vs. WAS	10/28/62	505
8	Elvis Grbac*	KC at OAK	11/05/00	504
9	Joe Namath	NYJ at BAC	9/24/72	496
10	Boomer Esiason	CIN at RAM	10/07/90	490
=	Tommy Kramer	MIN at WAS	11/02/86	490

Sonny Jurgensen is the only quarterback on this list who played prior to 1974, when the NFL began liberalizing its rules to encourage more passing. Jurgensen played 18 seasons for the Eagles (1957–1963) and the Redskins (1964–1974).

LAST BUT NOT LEAST

Five quarterbacks—John Elway, Todd Blackledge, Jim Kelly, Tony Eason, and Ken O'Brien—already had been selected in the first round as the Dolphins prepared to make the 1983 NFL Draft's twenty-seventh choice. Miami drafted University of Pittsburgh quarterback Dan Marino, and coach Don Shula quickly converted the Dolphins' run-oriented offense into a record-setting passing attack. Marino passed for an NFL-record 5,084 yards in his second season en route to a berth in Super Bowl XIX. Marino set 24 NFL records and posted a .613 winning percentage as a starter during his 17-year career.

TIME OUT

Active through 2001 season

QUARTERBACKS

MOST TOUCHDOWN PASSES, CAREER

	PLAYER	TDS
1	Dan Marino	420
2	Fran Tarkenton	342
3	John Elway	300
4	Warren Moon	291
5	Johnny Unitas	290
6	Brett Favre*	287
7	Joe Montana	273
8	Dave Krieg	261
9	Sonny Jurgensen	255
10	Dan Fouts	254

MOST TOUCHDOWN PASSES, SEASON

	PLAYER	TEAM	YEAR	TDS
1	Dan Marino	MIA	1984	48
2	Dan Marino	MIA	1986	44
3	Kurt Warner*	RAM	1999	41
4	Brett Favre*	GB	1996	39
5	Brett Favre*	GB	1995	38
6	George Blanda	HOU	1961	36
=	Y.A. Tittle	NYG	1963	36
=	Steve Young	SF	1998	36
=	Steve Beuerlein	CAR	1999	36
=	Kurt Warner*	RAM	2001	36

MOST GAMES WITH 4 OR MORE TOUCHDOWN PASSES, CAREER

	PLAYER	GAMES
1	Dan Marino	21
2	Johnny Unitas	17
3	Brett Favre*	14
4	George Blanda	13
5	Dan Fouts	12
=	Sonny Jurgensen	12
=	Fran Tarkenton	12
8	John Elway	10
=	Jim Kelly	10
10	Many tied with	9

MOST TOUCHDOWN PASSES, GAME

	PLAYER	TEAM VS OPP	DATE	TDS
1	Sid Luckman	CHI at NYG	11/14/43	7
=	Adrian Burk	PHI vs. WAS	10/17/54	7
=	George Blanda	HOU vs. NYT	11/19/61	7
=	Y.A. Tittle	NYG vs. WAS	10/28/62	7
=	Joe Kapp	MIN vs. BAC	9/28/69	7
6	Many tied with			6

MOST TOUCHDOWN PASSES, QUARTERBACK TO RECEIVER COMBINATION, CAREER

	QUARTERBACK TO RECEIVER	TEAM	YEARS	TDS
1	Steve Young to Jerry Rice*	SF	1987–1999	85
2	Dan Marino to Mark Clayton	MIA	1983–1992	79
3	Jim Kelly to Andre Reed	BUF	1986–1996	65
4	Johnny Unitas to Raymond Berry	BAC	1956–1967	63
5	Brett Favre* to Antonio Freeman*	GB	1995–2001	57
6	John Hadl to Lance Alworth	SD	1962–1970	56
7	Dan Marino to Mark Duper	MIA	1983–1992	55
=	Joe Montana to Jerry Rice*	SF	1985–1992	55
9	Sonny Jurgensen to Charley Taylor	WAS	1964–1974	53
10	Ken Anderson to Isaac Curtis	CIN	1973–1984	51

From 1983–1992, 46 percent of Dan Marino's touchdown passes were to either of the "Marks Brothers"—Mark Clayton or Mark Duper.

MAKING A NAME FOR HIMSELF

A Columbia graduate, the Bears' Sid Luckman passed for 7 touchdowns on "Sid Luckman Day" at the Polo Grounds as Chicago defeated the Giants 56-7 in 1943.

DID YOU KNOW?
Dan Marino has posted the two best single-season touchdown pass totals in league history, but he only led the league three times, and never after 1986, his fourth NFL season.

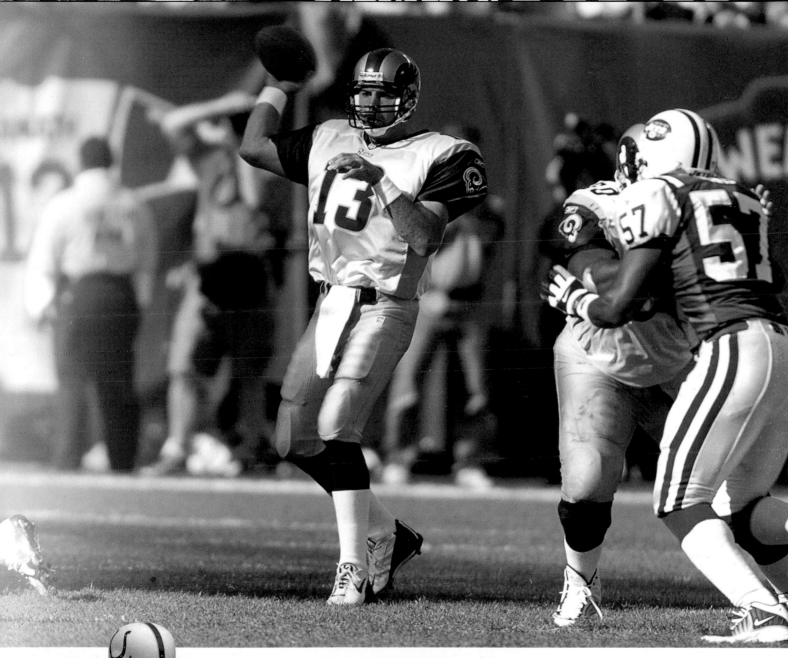

JOHNNY U

Johnny Unitas is the Joe DiMaggio of football. As nobody has come within 12 games of DiMaggio's 56-game hitting streak, Unitas's record of 47 consecutive games with a touchdown pass has proven equally unbreakable. Established more than 40 years ago, no player has even come within a season of breaking Unitas' mark. The streak began late in Unitas' first season with the Colts (1956), and ended in 1960. And Unitas averaged just 26 pass attempts a game during the streak, far fewer than most quarterbacks attempt in a game today.

TIME OUT

A REAL-LIFE FAIRY TALE
A former Arena League quarterback, 28-year-old Kurt Warner replaced an injured Trent Green during the 1999 preseason and led the Rams to the Super Bowl XXXIV title.

Active through 2001 season

HIGHEST PASSER RATING, CAREER#

PLAYER	RATING
1 Steve Young	96.8
2 Joe Montana	92.3
3 Brett Favre*	86.8
4 Dan Marino	86.4
5 Peyton Manning*	85.1
6 Mark Brunell*	85.0
7 Jim Kelly	84.4
8 Roger Staubach	83.4
9 Brad Johnson*	83.1
10 Rich Gannon*	83.1

#Minimum 1,500 attempts

HIGHEST PASSER RATING, SEASON

PLAYER	TEAM	YEAR	RATING
1 Steve Young	SF	1994	112.8
2 Joe Montana	SF	1989	112.4
3 Milt Plum	CLE	1960	110.4
4 Sammy Baugh	WAS	1945	109.9
5 Kurt Warner*	RAM	1999	109.2
6 Dan Marino	MIA	1984	108.9
7 Sid Luckman	CHI	1943	107.5
8 Steve Young	SF	1992	107.0
9 R. Cunningham*	MIN	1998	106.0
10 Bart Starr	GB	1966	105.0

NFL NOTEBOOK

Only Dan Marino had a better passer rating in his rookie season than Greg Cook. Who is Greg Cook? Selected with the fifth overall pick of the 1969 draft, Cook led the Cincinnati Bengals to a 3-0 start in 1969 before suffering an arm injury. Cook missed three games before coming back from the injury to guide the Bengals to their only other victory. But he missed the next three seasons while recovering from three shoulder surgeries. He attempted just 3 passes in the 1973 season opener before retiring.

HIGHEST COMPLETION PERCENTAGE, CAREER#

PLAYER	YEARS	COMP	ATT	PCT
1 Steve Young	1985–1999	2,667	4,149	64.28
2 Joe Montana	1979–1994	3,409	5,391	63.24
3 Brad Johnson*	1992–2001	1,466	2,380	61.60
4 Troy Aikman	1989–2000	2,898	4,715	61.46
5 Peyton Manning*	1998–2001	1,357	2,226	60.96
6 Brett Favre*	1991–2001	3,311	5,442	60.84
7 Mark Brunell*	1994–2001	1,897	3,145	60.32
8 Jim Kelly	1986–1996	2,874	4,779	60.14
9 Ken Stabler	1970–1984	2,270	3,793	59.85
10 Danny White	1976–1988	1,761	2,950	59.69

#Minimum 1,500 attempts

HIGHEST COMPLETION PERCENTAGE, SEASON

PLAYER	TEAM	YEAR	COMP	ATT	PCT
1 Ken Anderson	CIN	1982	218	309	70.55
2 Sammy Baugh	WAS	1945	128	182	70.33
3 Steve Young	SF	1994	324	461	70.28
4 Joe Montana	SF	1989	271	386	70.21
5 Troy Aikman	DAL	1993	271	392	69.13
6 Kurt Warner*	RAM	2001	375	546	68.68
7 Steve Young	SF	1993	314	462	67.97
8 Kurt Warner*	RAM	2000	235	347	67.72
9 Steve Young	SF	1996	214	316	67.72
10 Steve Young	SF	1997	241	356	67.70

SLINGIN' SAMMY

Sammy Baugh helped revolutionize pro football with his wide-open passing game. The Redskins moved from Boston to Washington, D.C., in 1937 and made Baugh their first-round selection. As a rookie, Baugh guided the Redskins to their first NFL championship. A gifted athlete, Baugh also punted and played defensive back throughout his 16-year career. In 1943, he led the NFL in passing, interceptions, and punting. He led the league in passing six times and still ranks as the NFL's all-time leading punter.

TIME OUT

DID YOU KNOW?
On December 26, 1993, Cleveland Browns quarterback Vinny Testaverde had the most accurate game in NFL history, completing 21 of 23 passes (91.3 percent).

BENGAL OF ANOTHER STRIPE

Augustana College's Ken Anderson is Cincinnati's all-time leader in passing yards and touchdown passes, and he guided the Bengals to Super Bowl XVI.

MOST YEARS LEADING LEAGUE IN PASSING

PLAYER	SEASONS
1 Sammy Baugh	6
= Steve Young	6
3 Len Dawson	4
= Roger Staubach	4
= Ken Anderson	4
6 Arnie Herber	3
= Norm Van Brocklin	3
= Bart Starr	3
9 Many tied with	2

Since 1973, the NFL passing champion has been determined by a complex formula that weighs accuracy, yards, touchdowns, and interceptions. Prior to that, the top passers were rated according to their league ranking in each category.

RATING MONSTER

Steve Young became the San Francisco 49ers' starting quarterback in 1991 and proceeded to lead the league in passer rating six of the next seven seasons.

* Active through 2001 season

QUARTERBACKS

WHAT MIGHT HAVE BEEN
Warren Moon's NFL passing numbers would be even more impressive if he had not played his first six seasons in the Canadian Football League.

MOST COMPLETIONS, CAREER

	PLAYER	COMP
1	Dan Marino	4,967
2	John Elway	4,123
3	Warren Moon	3,988
4	Fran Tarkenton	3,686
5	Joe Montana	3,409
6	Brett Favre*	3,311
7	Dan Fouts	3,297
8	Vinny Testaverde*	3,157
9	Dave Krieg	3,105
10	Boomer Esiason	2,969

Dan Marino averaged 20.5 completions per game during his 17-year career.

MOST COMPLETIONS, SEASON

	PLAYER	TEAM	YEAR	COMP
1	Warren Moon	HOU	1991	404
2	Drew Bledsoe*	NE	1994	400
3	Dan Marino	MIA	1994	385
4	Dan Marino	MIA	1986	378
5	Warren Moon	MIN	1995	377
6	Kurt Warner*	RAM	2001	375
7	Drew Bledsoe*	NE	1996	373
8	Warren Moon	MIN	1994	371
9	Brett Favre*	GB	1994	363
10	Dan Marino	MIA	1984	362
=	Warren Moon	HOU	1990	362

MOST 3,000-YARD PASSING SEASONS

	PLAYER	SEASONS
1	Dan Marino	13
2	John Elway	12
3	Brett Favre*	10
4	Warren Moon	9
5	Jim Kelly	8
=	Joe Montana	8
7	Drew Bledsoe*	7
=	Boomer Esiason	7
9	Dan Fouts	6
=	Dave Krieg	6
=	Phil Simms	6
=	Steve Young	6

TRIVIA TIME
In 1998, the Colts' Peyton Manning set NFL records for most completions (326), most attempts (575), and most passing yards (3,739) by a rookie. Whose records did Manning break?

A: Seattle's Rick Mirer (1993)

PASSING TOP 10

REBIRTH IN GREEN BAY

In the 24 seasons after the Packers' 1967 NFL championship, they won only 42 percent of their games. Since they traded for Brett Favre in 1992, Green Bay has won 66 percent of its games.

HIGHEST WINNING PERCENTAGE, ACTIVE STARTING QUARTERBACK#

	PLAYER	WINS	LOSSES	PCT
1	Kurt Warner*	35	8	.814
2	Jay Fiedler*	22	10	.688
3	Brett Favre*	103	54	.656
4	Donovan McNabb*	24	14	.632
5	Brad Johnson*	41	25	.621
6	Kordell Stewart*	43	27	.614
7	R. Cunningham*	82	52	.611
8	Steve McNair*	48	31	.608
9	Doug Flutie*	35	25	.583
10	Mark Brunell*	57	42	.576

#Minimum 30 starts
Cunningham's percentage includes one tie

MOST VICTORIES, ACTIVE STARTING QUARTERBACK

	PLAYER	WINS
1	Brett Favre*	103
2	Randall Cunningham*	82
3	Vinny Testaverde*	79
4	Drew Bledsoe*	63
5	Chris Chandler*	62
6	Rich Gannon*	61
7	Mark Brunell*	57
8	Neil O'Donnell*	54
9	Trent Dilfer*	49
10	Steve McNair*	48

Trent Dilfer entered the 2002 season with a 15-game winning streak (including playoffs).

MOST COMPLETIONS, GAME

	PLAYER	TEAM VS OPP	DATE	COMP
1	Drew Bledsoe*	NE vs. MIN	11/13/94	45
2	Richard Todd	NYJ vs. SF	9/21/80	42
=	Vinny Testaverde*	NYJ vs. SEA	12/6/98	42
4	Warren Moon	HOU vs. DAL	11/10/91	41
5	Ken Anderson	CIN at SD	12/20/82	40
=	Phil Simms	NYG at CIN	10/13/85	40
=	Brad Johnson*	TB vs. CHI	11/18/01	40
8	Dan Marino	MIA at BUF	11/16/86	39
=	Drew Bledsoe*	NE at PIT	12/16/95	39
=	Elvis Grbac*	KC at OAK	11/5/00	39

JOE COOL

How cool a quarterback was Joe Montana? He was so calm under pressure, none of his 122 career Super Bowl pass attempts were intercepted. Montana engineered 31 fourth-quarter comebacks, the most memorable of which was a 92-yard drive in the final 3:10 of Super Bowl XXIII against the Cincinnati Bengals that gave the San Francisco 49ers a 23-16 victory. Montana and the 49ers dominated the 1980s, winning four Super Bowls in a nine-year span. He returned from an elbow injury, which forced him to miss nearly all of the 1991 and 1992 seasons, to guide the Kansas City Chiefs to the playoffs his final two seasons (1993 and 1994), including a trip to the 1993 AFC Championship Game.

TIME OUT

*Active through 2001 season

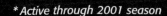

QUARTERBACKS

MOST PASS ATTEMPTS, CAREER

	PLAYER	ATT
1	Dan Marino	8,358
2	John Elway	7,250
3	Warren Moon	6,823
4	Fran Tarkenton	6,467
5	Vinny Testaverde*	5,644
6	Dan Fouts	5,604
7	Brett Favre*	5,442
8	Joe Montana	5,391
9	Dave Krieg	5,311
10	Boomer Esiason	5,205

Marino led the NFL in pass attempts five times during his career, the fifth time coming in 1997 when he was 36 years old.

MOST PASS ATTEMPTS, SEASON

	PLAYER	TEAM	YEAR	ATT
1	Drew Bledsoe*	NE	1994	691
2	Warren Moon	HOU	1991	655
3	Drew Bledsoe*	NE	1995	636
4	Dan Marino	MIA	1986	623
=	Drew Bledsoe*	NE	1996	623
6	Dan Marino	MIA	1994	615
7	Dan Fouts	SD	1981	609
8	Dan Marino	MIA	1988	606
=	Warren Moon	MIN	1995	606
10	John Elway	DEN	1985	605

The Patriots are not remembered as a pass-happy team, but from 1994 to 1996 Drew Bledsoe averaged more than 40 pass attempts per game, the most ever by a quarterback in a three-year span.

IF IT AIN'T BROKE, DON'T FIX IT
Drew Bledsoe attempted an NFL-record 70 passes, with no interceptions, as the Patriots defeated the Vikings 26-20 in overtime on November 13, 1994.

MOST PASS ATTEMPTS, GAME

	PLAYER	TEAM VS OPP	DATE	ATT
1	Drew Bledsoe*	NE vs. MIN	11/13/94	70
2	Vinny Testaverde*	NYJ at BAL	12/24/00	69
3	George Blanda	HOU at BUF	11/1/64	68
=	Jon Kitna*	CIN vs. PIT	12/30/01	68
5	Chris Miller	ATL vs. DET	12/24/89	66
6	Dan Marino	MIA at BUF	12/30/95	64
7	Rich Gannon*	MIN at NE	10/20/91	63
=	Vinny Testaverde*	NYJ vs. SEA	12/6/98	63
=	Elvis Grbac*	BAL at CIN	9/23/01	63
=	Chris Weinke*	CAR vs. ARI	12/30/01	63

24

DID YOU KNOW?
Prior to the Rick Mirer-Drew Bledsoe 1993 rookie class, the record for most pass attempts by a rookie in a season was held by Seattle's Jim Zorn with 439 attempts (1976).

LOWEST PERCENTAGE, PASSES INTERCEPTED, CAREER#

	PLAYER	ATT	INT	PCT
1	Neil O'Donnell*	3,197	67	2.10
2	Steve Bono	1,700	42	2.47
3	Mark Brunell*	1,719	43	2.51
4	Joe Montana	5,391	139	2.58
5	Steve Young	4,149	107	2.58
6	Bernie Kosar	3,365	87	2.59
7	Steve McNair*	2,288	61	2.67
8	Rich Gannon*	1,758	54	2.67
9	Ken O'Brien	3,602	98	2.72
10	Jeff Blake*	2,533	72	2.84

#Minimum 1,500 attempts

IRONY

Although he holds the NFL record for lowest percentage of passes intercepted, Neil O'Donnell was intercepted 3 times in Pittsburgh's Super Bowl XXX defeat.

HIGHEST AVERAGE GAIN PER PASS, CAREER#

	PLAYER	YEARS	ATT	YDS	AVG
1	Otto Graham	1950–1955	1,565	13,499	8.63
2	Sid Luckman	1939–1950	1,744	14,686	8.42
3	Norm Van Brocklin	1949–1960	2,895	23,611	8.16
4	Steve Young	1985–1998	4,065	32,678	7.98
5	Ed Brown	1954–1965	1,987	15,600	7.85
6	Bart Starr	1956–1971	3,149	24,718	7.85
7	Johnny Unitas	1956–1973	5,186	40,239	7.76
8	Earl Morrall	1956–1976	2,689	20,809	7.74
9	Dan Fouts	1973–1987	5,604	43,040	7.68
10	Len Dawson	1957–1975	3,741	28,711	7.67

#Minimum 1,500 attempts

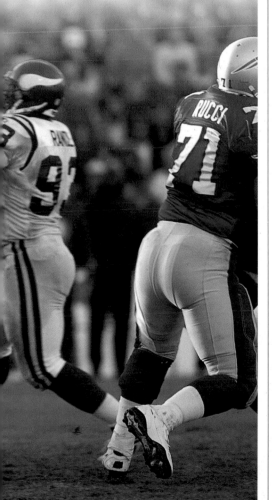

OTTOMATIC

The Cleveland Browns, led by quarterback Otto Graham, dominated the All-America Football Conference (AAFC) during that league's brief existence (1946–49). After winning all four AAFC crowns, Cleveland joined the NFL and rolled to six consecutive title games (1950–55), winning three. That left Graham, who retired after leading Cleveland to the 1955 NFL championship, with a perfect record—10 championship games in 10 pro seasons.

TIME OUT

Active through 2001 season

MOST TIMES SACKED, CAREER

PLAYER	SACKS
1 John Elway	516
2 Dave Krieg	494
3 Randall Cunningham*	484
4 Fran Tarkenton	483
5 Phil Simms	477
6 Warren Moon	458
7 Craig Morton	405
8 Ken Anderson	398
9 Archie Manning	396
10 Jim Plunkett	380

Six of the quarterbacks on this list (Elway, Tarkenton, Simms, Morton, Anderson, Plunkett) started a Super Bowl game. Elway and Plunkett each won two Super Bowls, and Simms won one.

MOST TIMES SACKED, SEASON

PLAYER	TEAM	YEAR	SACKS
1 R. Cunningham*	PHI	1986	72
2 Ken O'Brien	NYJ	1985	62
= Steve Beuerlein*	CAR	2000	62
4 Neil Lomax	STC	1985	61
5 R. Cunningham*	PHI	1992	60
6 Tony Eason	NE	1984	59
7 Don Meredith	DAL	1964	58
= Jeff George*	OAK	1997	58
9 R. Cunningham*	PHI	1988	57
= Mark Brunell*	JAX	2001	57

The assumption may be that the quarterbacks listed above played on bad teams, but the Eagles made the playoffs under Cunningham's guidance in 1988 and 1992, and the Jets were an AFC wild-card team in 1985.

BATTERED BUT NOT BRUISED
Despite being remembered for his elusiveness in the pocket, John Elway was sacked an NFL-record 516 times during his 16-year career.

MOST TIMES SACKED, GAME

PLAYER	TEAM VS OPP	DATE	SACKS
1 Bert Jones	BAC vs. STC	10/26/80	12
= Warren Moon	HOU vs. DAL	9/29/85	12
3 Charley Johnson	STC at NYG	11/1/64	11
= Bart Starr	GB vs. DET	11/7/65	11
= Jack Kemp	BUF vs. OAK	10/15/67	11
= Bob Berry	ATL at STC	11/24/68	11
= Greg Landry	DET vs. DAL	10/6/75	11
= Ron Jaworski	PHI at STC	12/18/83	11
= Paul McDonald	CLE at KC	9/30/84	11
= Archie Manning	MIN at CHI	10/28/84	11
= Steve Pelluer	DAL at SD	11/16/86	11
= Randall Cunningham*	PHI at RAI	11/30/86	11
= David Norrie	NYJ vs. DAL	10/4/87	11
= Troy Aikman	DAL vs. PHI	9/15/91	11
= Bernie Kosar	CLE at IND	9/6/92	11

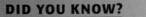

RECORD-SETTING CAREER

Upon his retirement after the 1978 season, Fran Tarkenton held NFL records for passing yards, touchdowns, completions, and attempts.

MOST TIMES INTERCEPTED, CAREER

	PLAYER	INT
1	George Blanda	277
2	John Hadl	268
3	Fran Tarkenton	266
4	Norm Snead	257
5	Johnny Unitas	253
6	Dan Marino	252
7	Jim Hart	247
8	Bobby Layne	243
9	Dan Fouts	242
10	Warren Moon	233

MOST TIMES INTERCEPTED, SEASON

	PLAYER	TEAM	YEAR	INT
1	George Blanda	HOU	1962	42
2	Vinny Testaverde*	TB	1988	35
3	Frank Tripucka	DEN	1960	34
4	John Hadl	SD	1968	32
=	Fran Tarkenton	MIN	1978	32
6	Sid Luckman	CHI	1947	31
7	Al Dorow	NYT	1961	30
=	George Blanda	HOU	1965	30
=	Jim Hart	STC	1967	30
=	Ken Stabler	OAK	1978	30
=	Richard Todd	NYJ	1980	30

Al Dorow led the AFL in touchdown passes in 1960 and interceptions in 1961, then was traded to Buffalo and attempted just 75 more passes the following season before retiring.

LOWEST WINNING PERCENTAGE, ACTIVE STARTING QUARTERACK[#]

	PLAYER	WINS	LOSSES	PCT
1	Tim Couch*	11	26	.297
2	Jake Plummer*	25	41	.379
3	Trent Green*	14	21	.400
4	Charlie Batch*	19	27	.413
5	Jeff Blake*	32	45	.416
6	Gus Frerotte*	25	33	.432
7	Tony Banks*	33	42	.440
8	Kent Graham*	17	21	.447
9	Vinny Testaverde*	79	98	.447
10	Scott Mitchell*	32	39	.451

[#]Minimum 30 starts
Percentages for Frerotte and Testaverde include one tie game each

MOST TIMES INTERCEPTED, GAME

	PLAYER	TEAM VS OPP	DATE	W/L	INT
1	Jim Hardy	CHC vs. PHI	9/24/50	L	8
2	Parker Hall	RAM at GB	11/8/42	L	7
=	Frank Sinkwich	DET vs. GB	10/24/43	L	7
=	Bob Waterfield	RAM at GB	10/17/48	L	7
=	Zeke Bratkowski	CHI at BAC	10/2/60	L	7
=	Tommy Wade	PIT vs. PHI	12/12/65	L	7
=	Ken Stabler	OAK vs. DEN	10/16/77	L	7
=	Steve DeBerg	TB vs. SF	9/7/86	L	7
=	Ty Detmer*	DET at CLE	9/23/01	L	7
10	Many tied with				6

DO I THROW OR DO I GO?

Randall Cunningham has rushed for more yards than any other quarterback in NFL history. But as a second-year quarterback in 1986, the fleet-footed Cunningham was sacked an NFL-record 72 times. Furthermore, Cunningham attempted just 209 passes and rushed 66 times in 1986, meaning he was sacked or scrambled nearly 40 percent of the time he dropped back to pass. The Eagles stayed with Cunningham, and within two seasons they posted the first of three consecutive postseason appearances.

TIME OUT

* Active through 2001 season

WIDE RECEIVERS

MOST RECEPTIONS, CAREER

	PLAYER	REC
1	Jerry Rice*	1,364
2	Cris Carter*	1,093
3	Andre Reed	951
4	Art Monk	940
5	Tim Brown*	937
6	Irving Fryar	851
7	Steve Largent	819
8	Henry Ellard	814
9	Larry Centers*	765
10	James Lofton	764

Larry Centers is the only running back on this list. He also holds the single-season mark for receptions by a running back (101 in 1995).

MOST RECEPTIONS, SEASON

	PLAYER	TEAM	YEAR	REC
1	Herman Moore*	DET	1995	123
2	Cris Carter*	MIN	1994	122
=	Jerry Rice*	SF	1995	122
=	Cris Carter*	MIN	1995	122
5	Isaac Bruce*	RAM	1995	119
6	Jimmy Smith*	JAX	1999	116
7	Marvin Harrison*	IND	1999	115
8	Rod Smith*	DEN	2001	113
9	Sterling Sharpe	GB	1993	112
=	Jerry Rice*	SF	1994	112
=	Jimmy Smith*	JAX	2001	112

Nine players had 100 or more receptions in 1995, including Herman Moore's teammate, Brett Perriman (108). Moore and Perriman's 231 catches are the most ever by two teammates in a season.

CATCHING RICE

Jerry Rice, the third receiver selected in the 1985 NFL Draft (after Al Toon and Eddie Brown), is the NFL's all-time leader in receptions, receiving yards, and touchdown catches.

TRIVIA TIME

Houston's Charley Hennigan caught a record 101 passes in 1964, a mark that lasted 20 years, until Washington's Art Monk caught 106 passes in 1984. Can you name the first player to catch 100 passes in a season?

A: Lionel Taylor caught 100 passes for Denver in 1961.

MOST RECEIVING YARDS, CAREER

	PLAYER	YARDS
1	Jerry Rice*	20,386
2	James Lofton	14,004
3	Cris Carter*	13,833
4	Henry Ellard	13,777
5	Tim Brown*	13,237
6	Andre Reed	13,198
7	Steve Largent	13,089
8	Irving Fryar	12,785
9	Art Monk	12,721
10	Charlie Joiner	12,146

James Lofton averaged 18.3 yards per catch, the highest average among the players on this list.

MOST RECEIVING YARDS, SEASON

	PLAYER	TEAM	YEAR	YDS
1	Jerry Rice*	SF	1995	1,848
2	Isaac Bruce*	RAM	1995	1,781
3	Charley Hennigan	HOU	1961	1,746
4	Herman Moore*	DET	1995	1,686
5	Marvin Harrison*	IND	1999	1,663
6	Jimmy Smith*	JAX	1999	1,636
7	Torry Holt*	RAM	2000	1,635
8	Michael Irvin	DAL	1995	1,603
9	Lance Alworth	SD	1965	1,602
=	Rod Smith*	DEN	2000	1,602

NOT A ONE-GAME WONDER

Tom Fears's 18-catch game in 1950 was not a fluke. Fears led the NFL in receptions three consecutive seasons (1948–1950) and made the game-winning 73-yard touchdown catch in the 1951 NFL title game.

MOST RECEPTIONS, GAME

	PLAYER	TEAM VS OPP	DATE	YARDS	REC
1	Terrell Owens*	SF vs. CHI	12/17/00	283	20
2	Tom Fears	RAM vs. GB	12/3/50	189	18
3	Clark Gaines	NYJ vs. SF	9/21/80	160	17
4	Sonny Randle	STC at NYG	11/4/62	256	16
=	Jerry Rice*	SF vs. RAM	11/20/94	165	16
=	Keenan McCardell*	JAX at RAM	10/20/96	232	16
7	Rickey Young	MIN at NE	12/16/79	116	15
=	William Andrews	ATL vs. PIT	11/15/81	124	15
=	Kellen Winslow	SD at GB	10/7/84	157	15
=	Steve Largent	SEA at DET	10/18/87	261	15
=	Flipper Anderson	RAM at NO	11/26/89	336	15
=	Andre Reed	BUF vs. GB	11/20/94	191	15
=	Isaac Bruce*	RAM vs. MIA	12/24/95	210	15
=	Jimmy Smith*	JAX at BAL	9/10/00	291	15

NFL NOTEBOOK

On December 17, 2000, San Francisco 49ers wide receiver Terrell Owens had 20 receptions to break Tom Fears's 50-year-old NFL record. Owens had 11 receptions in the first half, added a 27-yard touchdown catch in the third quarter, and broke the record with an 11-yard catch with four minutes remaining in the 49ers' 17-0 victory over the Chicago Bears.

* Active through 2001 season

WIDE RECEIVERS

MOST RECEIVING TOUCHDOWNS, SEASON

	PLAYER	TEAM	YEAR	TDS
1	Jerry Rice*	SF	1987	22
2	Mark Clayton	MIA	1984	18
=	Sterling Sharpe	GB	1994	18
4	Don Hutson	GB	1942	17
=	Elroy Hirsch	RAM	1951	17
=	Bill Groman	HOU	1961	17
=	Jerry Rice*	SF	1989	17
=	Cris Carter*	MIN	1995	17
=	Carl Pickens	CIN	1995	17
=	Randy Moss*	MIN	1998	17

Jerry Rice caught a touchdown pass in 13 consecutive games in 1986–87 to set an NFL record.

MOST RECEIVING TOUCHDOWNS, CAREER

	PLAYER	TDS
1	Jerry Rice*	185
2	Cris Carter*	129
3	Steve Largent	100
4	Don Hutson	99
5	Tim Brown*	95
6	Don Maynard	88
7	Andre Reed	87
8	Paul Warfield	85
=	Lance Alworth	85
10	Mark Clayton	84
=	Irving Fryar	84
=	Tommy McDonald	84
=	Andre Rison	84

BIG PLAY RANDY

Randy Moss set an NFL rookie record by catching 17 touchdown passes in 1998, shattering the previous mark of 13. Of Moss's 17 touchdown catches, 10 were in excess of 40 yards.

TRIVIA TIME
Terry Glenn holds the record for most receptions by a rookie. He had 90 catches for the Patriots in 1996. Whose record did Glenn break?

A: The 49ers' Earl Cooper, who had 83 catches in 1980.

LONGEST PASS RECEPTION

	PLAYERS	TEAM VS OPP	DATE	YARDS
1	Andy Farkas from Frank Filchock	WAS vs. PIT	10/15/39	99
=	Bobby Mitchell from George Izo	WAS at CLE	9/15/63	99
=	Pat Studstill from Karl Sweetan	DET at BAC	10/16/66	99
=	Gerry Allen from Sonny Jurgensen	WAS at CHI	9/15/68	99
=	Cliff Branch from Jim Plunkett	RAI at WAS	10/2/83	99
=	Mike Quick from Ron Jaworski	PHI vs. ATL	11/10/85	99
=	Tony Martin* from Stan Humphries	SD at SEA	9/18/94	99
=	Robert Brooks from Brett Favre*	GB at CHI	9/11/95	99
9	Eight tied with			98

Amazingly, one of the eight 98-yard passes did not result in a touchdown. On Decemeber 10, 1972, the St. Louis Cardinals were pinned at their 1-yard line when quarterback Jim Hart fired a pass to Bobby Moore, who went the length of the field before being tackled at the Los Angeles Rams' 1-yard line. The Cardinals scored a touchdown on the next play en route to a 24-14 victory. As for Moore, today he is better known for his work on television as broadcaster Ahmad Rashad.

MOST RECEIVING YARDS, GAME

	PLAYER	TEAM VS OPP	DATE	REC	YARDS
1	Flipper Anderson	RAM at NO	11/26/89	15	336
2	Stephone Paige	KC vs. SD	12/22/85	8	309
3	Jim Benton	RAM at DET	11/22/45	10	303
4	Cloyce Box	DET at BAC	12/3/50	12	302
5	Jimmy Smith	JAX at BAL	9/10/00	15	291
6	Jerry Rice*	SF vs. MIN	12/18/95	14	289
7	John Taylor	SF at RAM	12/11/89	11	286
8	Terrell Owens*	SF vs. CHI	12/17/00	20	283
9	Charley Hennigan	HOU at BOS	10/13/61	13	272
10	Del Shofner	NYG vs. WAS	10/28/62	11	269

Jimmy Smith's performance came against the 2000 Ravens, one of the best defenses ever.

RACKING UP THE YARDS

Not only did Bill Groman tally a rookie record 1,473 receiving yards in 1960, he did it while playing a 14-game schedule—an average of 105 yards per game.

MOST SEASONS, 50 OR MORE RECEPTIONS

	PLAYER	SEASONS
1	Jerry Rice*	15
2	Andre Reed	13
3	Cris Carter*	11
4	Larry Centers*	10
=	Gary Clark	10
=	Henry Ellard	10
=	Steve Largent	10
8	Tim Brown*	9
=	James Lofton	9
=	Art Monk	9
=	Shannon Sharpe*	9

Jerry Rice has failed to reach 50 receptions only twice in 17 seasons.

NFL NOTEBOOK

In 2001, Cris Carter tied Jerry Rice's record of 11 consecutive seasons with at least 50 receptions. Larry Centers (10 seasons) and Tim Brown (9 seasons) also enter 2002 with active streaks.

THE BEST IN HIS ERA

No receiver dominated the game like Don Hutson did. In an era when the forward pass was an afterthought, the Pro Football Hall of Fame inductee set records by leading the NFL in receiving yards seven times, receptions eight times, and receiving touchdowns nine times during his 11-year career (1935–1945). His finest season was in 1942, when Hutson led the league with 74 catches—the next best player had 27. Hutson scored 17 touchdowns (second place had 9) and accumulated 1,211 receiving yards (compared to 345 for second place).

TIME OUT

*Active through 2001 season

WIDE RECEIVERS

MOST 100-YARD RECEIVING GAMES, CAREER

PLAYER	GAMES
1 Jerry Rice*	68
2 Don Maynard	50
3 Michael Irvin	47
4 James Lofton	43
5 Cris Carter*	42
6 Lance Alworth	41
= Tim Brown*	41
8 Steve Largent	40
9 Stanley Morgan	38
10 Henry Ellard	37

Maynard and Alworth are the only two players on this list who played prior to 1975.

QUITE A CATCH
Seattle acquired Steve Largent (number 80, below) from Houston in 1977 for an eighth-round draft choice. He went on to become one of the NFL's all-time great receivers.

MOST 100-YARD RECEIVING GAMES, SEASON

PLAYER	TEAM	YEAR	GMS
1 Michael Irvin	DAL	1995	11
2 Charley Hennigan	HOU	1961	10
= Herman Moore*	DET	1995	10
4 Elroy Hirsch	RAM	1951	9
= Bill Groman	HOU	1960	9
= Lance Alworth	SD	1965	9
= Don Maynard	NYJ	1967	9
= Stanley Morgan	NE	1986	9
= Mark Carrier	TB	1989	9
= Robert Brooks	GB	1995	9
= Isaac Bruce*	RAM	1995	9
= Jerry Rice*	SF	1995	9
= Marvin Harrison*	IND	1999	9
= Jimmy Smith*	JAX	1999	9
= David Boston*	ARI	2001	9

MOST CONSECUTIVE 100-YARD RECEIVING GAMES

PLAYER	TEAM	YEAR(S)	GMS
1 Charley Hennigan	HOU	1961	7
= Michael Irvin	DAL	1995	7
3 Raymond Berry	BAL	1960	6
= Bill Groman	HOU	1961	6
= Pat Studstill	DET	1966	6
= Isaac Bruce*	RAM	1995	6
7 Elroy Hirsch	RAM	1951	5
= Bob Boyd	RAM	1954	5
= Terry Barr	DET	1963	5
= Lance Alworth	SD	1966	5
= Don Maynard	NYJ	1968–69	5
= Harold Jackson	PHI	1971–72	5
= Patrick Jeffers*	CAR	1999	5

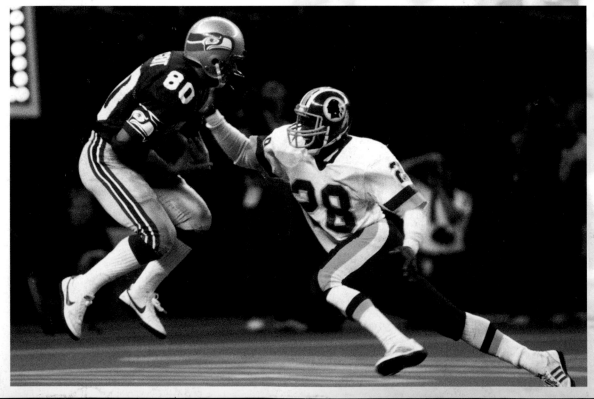

AIRBORNE COWBOYS
With Emmitt Smith in the backfield, Dallas is not thought of as a passing team. But Michael Irvin's 11 100-yard receiving games in 1995 established an NFL record.

DID YOU KNOW?
St. Louis Rams receiver Torry Holt set the single-game highest average reception mark in a September, 2000 game against Atlanta—he averaged 63 yards per catch (3 for 189 yards).

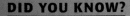

HIGHEST AVERAGE YARDS PER RECEPTION, CAREER#

	PLAYER	YEARS	REC	YDS	AVG
1	Homer Jones	1964–1970	224	4,986	22.3
2	Buddy Dial	1959–1966	261	5,436	20.8
3	Harlon Hill	1954–1962	233	4,717	20.2
4	Flipper Anderson	1988–1997	267	5,357	20.1
5	Paul Warfield	1964–1977	427	8,565	20.1
6	Bob Hayes	1965–1975	371	7,414	20.0
7	Willie Gault	1983–1993	333	6,635	19.9
8	Jimmy Orr	1958–1970	400	7,914	19.8
9	Ray Renfro	1952–1963	281	5,508	19.6
10	Hugh Taylor	1947–1954	272	5,233	19.2

#Minimum 200 receptions

HIGHEST AVERAGE YARDS PER RECEPTION, SEASON

	PLAYER	TEAM	YEAR	REC	YDS	AVG
1	Don Currivan	BOY	1947	24	782	32.6
2	Bucky Pope	RAM	1964	25	786	31.4
3	Bobby Duckworth	SD	1984	25	715	28.6
4	Jimmy Orr	PIT	1958	33	910	27.6
5	Homer Jones	NYG	1965	26	709	27.3
6	Elbert Dubenion	BUF	1964	42	1,139	27.1
7	Warren Wells	OAK	1969	47	1,260	26.8
8	Jack Snow	RAM	1967	28	735	26.3
9	Bob Hayes	DAL	1970	34	889	26.1
10	Ron Sellers	BOS	1969	27	705	26.1

After Pope's 1964 rookie season, he had just 9 receptions the rest of his career.

BOMBS AWAY

No player epitomized the high-flying and high-scoring AFL more than Lance Alworth. Nicknamed "Bambi" for his graceful strides and leaping ability, Alworth never scored fewer than 9 touchdowns or averaged less than 18.9 yards per catch during a remarkable stretch of six seasons (1963–68). Alworth led the AFL in touchdowns for three consecutive seasons (1964–66) and in 1978 became the first AFL player to be inducted into the Pro Football Hall of Fame.

TIME OUT

NFL NOTEBOOK

The last player to lead the NFL in receiving yards while averaging more than 20 yards per reception was Mike Quick, who totaled 1,409 yards on 69 receptions (an average of 20.4 yards per catch) for the Philadelphia Eagles in 1983.

Active through 2001 season

DEFENSE

MOST INTERCEPTIONS, CAREER

	PLAYER	INT
1	Paul Krause	81
2	Emlen Tunnell	79
3	Dick Lane	68
4	Ken Riley	65
5	Ronnie Lott	63
6	Dave Brown	62
=	Dick LeBeau	62
8	Rod Woodson*	61
9	Emmitt Thomas	58
10	Mel Blount	57
=	Bobby Boyd	57
=	Eugene Robinson*	57
=	Johnny Robinson	57
=	Everson Walls	57

Dick LeBeau became head coach of the Cincinnati Bengals in 2000, while Emmitt Thomas has been an NFL defensive coordinator since 1995.

MOST INTERCEPTIONS, SEASON

	PLAYER	TEAM	YEAR	INT
1	Dick Lane	RAM	1952	14
2	Dan Sandifer	WAS	1948	13
=	Spec Sanders	NYY	1950	13
=	Lester Hayes	OAK	1980	13
5	Bob Nussbaumer	CHC	1949	12
=	Don Doll	DET	1950	12
=	Woodley Lewis	RAM	1950	12
=	Jack Christiansen	DET	1953	12
=	Fred Glick	HOU	1963	12
=	Paul Krause	WAS	1964	12
=	Dainard Paulson	NYJ	1964	12
=	Emmitt Thomas	KC	1974	12
=	Mike Reinfeldt	HOU	1979	12

MAINTAINING A FAST START
Safety Paul Krause intercepted 2 passes in his first game, 12 his rookie season, and went on to establish an NFL record with 81 career interceptions.

DID YOU KNOW?
Bill Bradley (Philadelphia, 1971–72) and Everson Walls (Dallas, 1981–82) are the only two players in NFL history to lead the league in interceptions in back-to-back seasons.

MOST INTERCEPTION RETURN YARDS, SEASON

	PLAYER	TEAM	YEAR	YDS
1	Charlie McNeil	SD	1961	349
2	Deion Sanders	SF	1994	303
3	Don Doll	DET	1949	301
4	Dick Lane	RAM	1952	298
5	Bob Suci	BOS	1963	277
6	Woodley Lewis	RAM	1950	275
7	Mark McMillian	KC	1997	274
8	Lester Hayes	OAK	1980	273
9	Miller Farr	HOU	1967	264
10	Henry Jones	BUF	1992	263

Deion Sanders averaged 50.3 yards on his 6 interceptions in 1994, including 3 he returned for touchdowns.

MOST INTERCEPTIONS, GAME

	PLAYER	TEAM VS OPP	DATE	INT
1	Sammy Baugh	WAS vs. DET	11/14/43	4
=	Dan Sandifer	WAS vs. BOY	10/31/48	4
=	Don Doll	DET at CHC	10/23/49	4
=	Bob Nussbaumer	CHC at NYY	11/13/49	4
=	Russ Craft	PHI at CHC	9/24/50	4
=	Bobby Dillon	GB at DET	11/26/53	4
=	Jack Butler	PIT at WAS	12/13/53	4
=	Austin Gonsoulin	DEN at BUF	9/18/60	4
=	Jerry Norton	STC at WAS	11/20/60	4
=	Dave Baker	SF at RAM	12/4/60	4
=	Jerry Norton	STC at PIT	11/26/61	4
=	Bobby Ply	DAT vs. SD	12/16/62	4
=	Bobby Hunt	KC vs. HOU	10/4/64	4
=	Willie Brown	DEN vs. NYJ	11/15/64	4
=	Dick Anderson	MIA vs. PIT	12/3/73	4
=	Willie Buchanon	GB at SD	9/24/78	4
=	Deron Cherry	KC vs. SEA	9/29/85	4
=	Kwamie Lassiter*	ARI vs. SD	12/27/98	4
=	Deltha O'Neal*	DEN vs. KC	10/7/01	4

After an injury ended Jack Butler's career in 1959, he became the director of BLESTO, an NFL scouting service that currently shares information among 13 teams and is the most visible scouting service in the country.

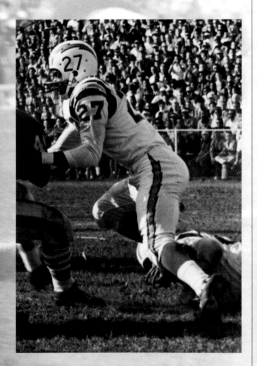

MCNEIL'S BIG SEASON

Charlie McNeil was in the right place at the right time in 1961. His 349 return yards (on 9 interceptions) that season set an NFL record. McNeil recorded just 10 interceptions during the rest of his four-year career, retiring after the 1964 season.

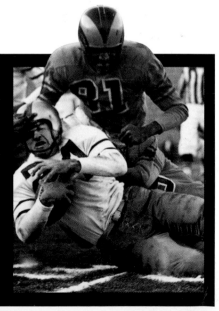

TIME OUT — THE PERFECT SWITCH

Army veteran Dick Lane walked into the Rams' office in 1952, displayed his press clippings from his junior college days in Nebraska, and asked for a tryout. The Rams took a chance on Lane and tried him at wide receiver. However, the Rams had two future Pro Football Hall of Fame receivers (Tom Fears and Elroy Hirsch) on their team. Lane was moved to cornerback, and he not only made the team, he intercepted 14 passes his rookie season—a record that still stands 50 years later. Lane's 68 career interceptions rank third all time, and he was inducted into the Pro Football Hall of Fame in 1974.

*Active through 2001 season

DEFENSE

MOST INTERCEPTION RETURN TOUCHDOWNS, CAREER

PLAYER	TDS
1 Rod Woodson*	10
2 Ken Houston	9
3 Eric Allen*	8
= Deion Sanders	8
5 Herb Adderley	7
= Erich Barnes	7
= Lem Barney	7
= Otis Smith	7
9 Bobby Bell	6
= Miller Farr	6
= Darrell Green*	6
= Tom Janik	6
= Aeneas Williams*	6

ADAPTING TO CHANGE
Rod Woodson, who played cornerback for 12 seasons before moving to safety in 1999, has an NFL-record 10 interception returns for touchdowns.

TRAIL BLAZER
Emlen Tunnell became the first African-American and first purely defensive player enshrined in the Pro Football Hall of Fame upon his 1967 induction.

TRIVIA TIME
Ronnie Lott is one of only two rookies in NFL history to return 3 interceptions for touchdowns in a single season. Can you name the other?

A: Lem Barney

MOST INTERCEPTION RETURN YARDS, CAREER

PLAYER	YARDS
1 Emlen Tunnell	1,282
2 Rod Woodson*	1,240
3 Dick Lane	1,207
4 Deion Sanders	1,187
5 Paul Krause	1,185
6 Lem Barney	1,077
7 Herb Adderley	1,046
8 Bobby Boyd	994
9 Bobby Dillon	976
10 Glen Edwards	961

MOST INTERCEPTION RETURN TOUCHDOWNS, SEASON

PLAYER	TEAM	YEAR	TDS
1 Ken Houston	HOU	1971	4
= Jim Kearney	KC	1972	4
= Eric Allen*	PHI	1993	4
4 Dick Harris	SD	1961	3
= Dick Lynch	NYG	1963	3
= Herb Adderley	GB	1965	3
= Lem Barney	DET	1967	3
= Miller Farr	HOU	1967	3
= Monte Jackson	RAM	1976	3
= Rod Perry	RAM	1978	3
= Ronnie Lott	SF	1981	3
= Lloyd Burruss	KC	1986	3
= Wayne Haddix	TB	1990	3
= Robert Massey	PHX	1992	3
= Ray Buchanan*	IND	1994	3
= Deion Sanders	SF	1994	3
= Mark McMillian	KC	1997	3
= Otis Smith*	NYJ	1997	3
= Jimmy Hitchcock	MIN	1998	3
= Eric Allen*	OAK	2000	3

MOST INTERCEPTION RETURN TOUCHDOWNS, GAME

PLAYER	TEAM VS OPP	DATE	TDS
1 Bill Blackburn	CHC vs. BOY	10/24/48	2
= Dan Sandifer	WAS vs. BOY	10/31/48	2
= Bob Franklin	CLE vs. CHI	12/11/60	2
= Bill Stacy	STC at DAL	11/5/61	2
= Jerry Norton	STC at PIT	11/26/61	2
= Miller Farr	HOU vs. BUF	12/7/68	2
= Ken Houston	HOU vs. SD	12/19/71	2
= Jim Kearney	KC at DEN	10/1/72	2
= Lemar Parrish	CIN at HOU	12/17/72	2
= Dick Anderson	MIA vs. PIT	12/3/73	2
= Prentice McCray	NE at NYJ	11/21/76	2
= Kenny Johnson	ATL vs. GB	11/27/83	2
= Mike Kozlowski	MIA vs. NYJ	12/16/83	2
= Dave Brown	SEA vs. KC	11/4/84	2
= Lloyd Burruss	KC vs. SD	10/19/86	2
= Henry Jones	BUF vs. IND	9/20/92	2
= Robert Massey	PHX vs. WAS	10/4/92	2
= Eric Allen*	PHI vs. NO	12/26/93	2
= Ken Norton	SF at RAM	10/22/95	2
= Otis Smith*	NYJ vs. TB	12/14/97	2
= Dewayne Washington*	PIT vs. JAX	11/22/98	2

The Boston Yanks were victimized by the first two players listed above—in back-to-back weeks. They lost the games 49-27 and 59-21. Jerry Norton, who was the only player with 2 interception returns for touchdowns in a losing cause, is also the only player in NFL history with two 4-interception games.

ONE OF THE BEST

Ken Houston was selected to the Pro Bowl 12 times during his 14-year career. Houston intercepted 49 passes, returning 9 for touchdowns, and recovered 19 opponents' fumbles. But he was not just an opportunist—Houston also was a strong tackler and an extremely intelligent player. It was no surprise that Houston was a first-ballot Pro Football Hall of Fame inductee in 1986.

TIME OUT

*Active through 2001 season

DEFENSE

FREAKY NUMBERS

Jevon Kearse's remarkable athletic ability earned him the nickname "Freak." All that talent translated into a dominating rookie season.

MOST SACKS, ROOKIE SEASON

	PLAYER	TEAM	YEAR	SACKS
1	Jevon Kearse*	TEN	1999	14.5
2	Leslie O'Neal	SD	1986	12.5
=	Simeon Rice*	ARI	1996	12.5
4	Charles Haley	SF	1986	12.0
5	Peter Boulware*	BAL	1997	11.5
6	Vernon Maxwell	BAC	1983	11.0
=	Darren Howard*	NO	2000	11.0
8	Greg Townsend	RAI	1983	10.5
=	Anthony Smith	RAI	1991	10.5
=	Dana Stubblefield*	SF	1993	10.5

The rookie performances of Jevon Kearse and Greg Townsend helped their teams capture AFC championships, with Townsend's Raiders going on to win Super Bowl XVIII.

DID YOU KNOW?
Mark Gastineau (1983–84) and Reggie White (1987–88) are the only two players to lead the NFL in sacks in consecutive seasons.

MOST SACKS, SEASON

	PLAYER	TEAM	YEAR	SACKS
1	Michael Strahan*	NYG	2001	22.5
2	Mark Gastineau	NYJ	1984	22.0
3	Reggie White	PHI	1987	21.0
=	Chris Doleman	MIN	1989	21.0
5	Lawrence Taylor	NYG	1986	20.5
6	Derrick Thomas	KC	1990	20.0
7	Tim Harris	GB	1989	19.5
8	Mark Gastineau	NYJ	1983	19.0
=	Bruce Smith*	BUF	1990	19.0
=	Clyde Simmons	PHI	1992	19.0

MOST SACKS, CAREER

	PLAYER	SACKS
1	Reggie White	198.0
2	Bruce Smith*	186.0
3	Kevin Greene	160.0
4	Chris Doleman	150.5
5	Richard Dent	137.5
6	Leslie O'Neal	132.5
=	Lawrence Taylor	132.5
8	Rickey Jackson	128.0
9	Derrick Thomas	126.5
10	John Randle*	125.0

MOST SACKS, GAME

	PLAYER	TEAM VS OPP	DATE	SACKS
1	Derrick Thomas	KC vs. SEA	11/11/90	7.0
2	Fred Dean	SF vs. NO	11/13/83	6.0
=	Derrick Thomas	KC vs. OAK	9/6/98	6.0
4	William Gay	DET at TB	9/4/83	5.5
5	Howie Long	RAI at WAS	10/2/83	5.0
=	Randy Holloway	MIN vs. ATL	9/16/84	5.0
=	Jim Jeffcoat	DAL at WAS	11/10/85	5.0
=	Leslie O'Neal	SD vs. DAL	11/16/86	5.0
=	Gary Jeter	RAM at RAI	9/18/88	5.0
=	Chuck Smith	ATL at NO	10/12/97	5.0

Despite Derrick Thomas's 7 sacks, the Chiefs lost 17-16 to the Seahawks.

DEFINING THE ART

David (Deacon) Jones played as good a game as he talked. The Rams' voluble defensive end coined the term "sack" to describe what he did to quarterbacks. Although sacks did not become an official statistic until 1982, Jones was unofficially credited with 173½ sacks during his 14-year career (1961–1974).

MOST SEASONS, 10 OR MORE SACKS

	PLAYER	SEASONS
1	Bruce Smith*	13
2	Reggie White	12
3	Kevin Greene	10
4	John Randle*	9
5	Richard Dent	8
=	Chris Doleman	8
=	Leslie O'Neal	8
8	Lawrence Taylor	7
=	Derrick Thomas	7
=	Greg Townsend	7

TIME OUT

THE MINISTER OF DEFENSE

Since the NFL began recording sacks, no player has wrapped up more quarterbacks than defensive end Reggie White. He recorded 198 sacks during his 15-year NFL career, and he added another 23½ sacks during two seasons in the USFL. An ordained minister off the field, White was dubbed "The Minister of Defense." He led the NFL with 21 sacks in just 12 games during the strike-shortened 1987 season, and was still such a force at the age of 37 that he won NFL defensive player of the year honors with the Green Bay Packers in 1998.

OFFENSE

MOST POINTS, CAREER

	PLAYER	PTS
1	Gary Anderson*	2,133
2	Morten Andersen*	2,036
3	George Blanda	2,002
4	Norm Johnson	1,736
5	Nick Lowery	1,711
6	Jan Stenerud	1,699
7	Eddie Murray	1,594
8	Al Del Greco	1,584
9	Pat Leahy	1,470
10	Jim Turner	1,439

Gary Anderson and Morten Andersen, who rank first and second in scoring in NFL history, both were drafted in 1982, played with their first team for 13 seasons (Gary with Pittsburgh, Morten with New Orleans), and were born in foreign countries (Gary in South Africa and Morten in Denmark).

MOST POINTS, SEASON

	PLAYER	TEAM	YEAR	PTS
1	Paul Hornung	GB	1960	176
2	Gary Anderson*	MIN	1998	164
3	Mark Moseley	WAS	1983	161
4	Marshall Faulk*	RAM	2000	160
5	Gino Cappelletti	BOS	1964	155
6	Emmitt Smith*	DAL	1995	150
7	Chip Lohmiller	WAS	1991	149
8	Gino Cappelletti	BOS	1961	147
9	Paul Hornung	GB	1961	146
10	Jim Turner	NYJ	1968	145
=	John Kasay*	CAR	1996	145
=	Mike Vanderjagt*	IND	1999	145

THE PERFECT REGULAR SEASON
During the 1998 regular season, Gary Anderson made all 94 of his kicking attempts (59 extra points, 35 field goals) for the Minnesota Vikings.

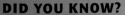

DID YOU KNOW?
Only six rookies have led the NFL in scoring: Doak Walker (1950); Gale Sayers (1965); Chester Marcol (1972); Frank Corral (1978); Marcus Allen (1982); and Kevin Butler (1985).

MOST SEASONS, 100 OR MORE POINTS

PLAYER	SEASONS
1 Gary Anderson*	13
2 Morten Andersen*	12
3 Nick Lowery	11
4 Jason Elam*	9
= Norm Johnson	9
= Pete Stoyanovich*	9
7 Steve Christie*	8
= Al Del Greco	8
9 Jan Stenerud	7
10 Many tied with	6

THE MORT REPORT
During his 19-year career, Morten Andersen has made 39 of his 81 field-goal attempts (48 percent) from 50 yards or more.

MOST POINTS, NO TOUCHDOWNS, SEASON

PLAYER	TEAM	YEAR	PTS
1 Gary Anderson*	MIN	1998	164
2 Mark Moseley	WAS	1983	161
3 Chip Lohmiller	WAS	1991	149
4 Jim Turner	NYJ	1968	145
= John Kasay*	CAR	1996	145
= Mike Vanderjagt*	IND	1999	145
7 Kevin Butler	CHI	1985	144
= Olindo Mare*	MIA	1999	144
9 Norm Johnson	PIT	1995	141
10 Steve Christie*	BUF	1998	140

Jim Turner scored his 145 points in only 14 games.

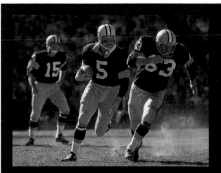

SCORING MACHINE

The standards set by Paul Hornung during the 1960 season may never be matched. The multitalented Hornung (number 5, left) led the NFL with 13 rushing touchdowns, caught 2 touchdown passes, and passed for 2 touchdowns. Hornung also served as the Packers' kicker, making 15 field goals and all 41 of his extra-point attempts. Hornung's total of 176 points established an NFL record. Hornung also led the league in points in 1959 and 1961, and was inducted into the Pro Football Hall of Fame in 1986.

TIME OUT

NFL NOTEBOOK

All of the top 10 scorers are kickers. Receiver Jerry Rice leads nonkickers with 1,184 points (through 2001), though his total ranks only twenty-second overall. No other nonkicker has more than 1,000 points, though Emmitt Smith is close with 956 points (through 2001).

* Active through 2001 season

MOST TOUCHDOWNS, CAREER

PLAYER	TDS
1 Jerry Rice*	196
2 Emmitt Smith*	159
3 Marcus Allen	145
4 Cris Carter*	130
5 Jim Brown	126
6 Walter Payton	125
7 John Riggins	116
8 Lenny Moore	113
9 Marshall Faulk*	110
10 Barry Sanders	109

Marshall Faulk vaulted into the NFL's top 10 for career touchdowns by scoring 47 touchdowns during the past two seasons (2000–01). Faulk's 47 touchdowns tied the two-year high established by Emmitt Smith in 1994–95. The best three-year total of 62 touchdowns was set by Smith from 1994–96.

NFL NOTEBOOK

Jim Brown set the standard by scoring 126 touchdowns in nine seasons (1957–1965), a record that stood for nearly 30 years. Though four players have surpassed his mark, no NFL player can match Brown's productivity—he is the only man to average better than a touchdown per game during his career (126 touchdowns in 118 games).

MARSHALL LAW

Marshall Faulk pierced the end zone 18 times via the ground and hauled in 8 touchdown receptions during his record-breaking 2000 season. He scored 4 touchdowns in three different games that year.

DID YOU KNOW?
In addition to scoring 15 touchdowns during his rookie season in 1962, running back Cookie Gilchrist also kicked 8 field goals and made 14 extra-point attempts for the Buffalo Bills.

DO YOU KNOW THIS MAN?

Nobody has seriously challenged Lenny Moore's record of scoring touchdowns in 18 consecutive games (second is O.J. Simpson with 14). Still, Moore remains one of the most underrated players in NFL history.

MOST TOUCHDOWNS, SEASON

	PLAYER	TEAM	YEAR	TDS
1	Marshall Faulk*	RAM	2000	26
2	Emmitt Smith*	DAL	1995	25
3	John Riggins	WAS	1983	24
4	O.J. Simpson	BUF	1975	23
=	Jerry Rice*	SF	1987	23
=	Terrell Davis*	DEN	1998	23
7	Gale Sayers	CHI	1965	22
=	Chuck Foreman	MIN	1975	22
=	Emmitt Smith*	DAL	1994	22
10	Jim Brown	CLE	1965	21
=	Joe Morris	NYG	1985	21
=	Terry Allen*	WAS	1996	21
=	Marshall Faulk*	RAM	2001	21

MOST TOUCHDOWNS, ROOKIE SEASON

	PLAYER	TEAM	YEAR	TDS
1	Gale Sayers	CHI	1965	22
2	Eric Dickerson	RAM	1983	20
3	Randy Moss*	MIN	1998	17
=	Fred Taylor*	JAX	1998	17
=	Edgerrin James*	IND	1999	17
6	Billy Sims	DET	1980	16
7	Cookie Gilchrist	BUF	1962	15
=	Ickey Woods	CIN	1988	15
=	Curtis Martin*	NE	1995	15
10	Marcus Allen	RAI	1982	14
=	Curt Warner	SEA	1983	14
=	Herschel Walker	DAL	1985	14
=	Barry Sanders	DET	1989	14

MOST TOUCHDOWNS, GAME

	PLAYER	TEAM	DATE	TDS
1	Ernie Nevers	CHC	11/28/29	6
=	Dub Jones	CLE	11/25/51	6
=	Gale Sayers	CHI	12/12/65	6
4	Bob Shaw	CHC	10/2/50	5
=	Jim Brown	CLE	11/1/59	5
=	Abner Haynes	DAT	11/26/61	5
=	Billy Cannon	HOU	12/10/61	5
=	Cookie Gilchrist	BUF	12/8/63	5
=	Paul Hornung	GB	12/12/65	5
=	Kellen Winslow	SD	11/22/81	5
=	Jerry Rice*	SF	10/14/90	5
=	James Stewart*	JAX	10/12/97	5

* Active through 2001 season

KICKERS

MOST FIELD GOALS, CAREER

PLAYER	FGS
1 Gary Anderson*	476
2 Morten Andersen*	464
3 Nick Lowery	383
4 Jan Stenerud	373
5 Norm Johnson	366
6 Eddie Murray	352
7 Al Del Greco	347
8 George Blanda	335
9 Pat Leahy	304
= Jim Turner	304

MOST FIELD GOALS, SEASON

PLAYER	TEAM	YEAR	FGS
1 Olindo Mare*	MIA	1999	39
2 John Kasay*	CAR	1996	37
3 Cary Blanchard	IND	1996	36
= Al Del Greco	TEN	1998	36
5 Ali Haji-Sheikh	NYG	1983	35
= Jeff Jaeger	RAI	1993	35
= Gary Anderson*	MIN	1998	35
= Matt Stover*	BAL	2000	35
9 Many tied with			34

NFL NOTEBOOK
Of Steve Cox's 6 career field goals, 4 were at least 55 yards. Cox, who was the Browns' punter, was only utilized in long field-goal situations. The 60- and 58-yard field goals made by Cox were his only successful field goals during the 1984 and 1983 seasons, respectively. Later in his career, Cox made kicks of 55 and 57 yards.

PERSEVERANCE PAYS OFF
Olindo Mare, the NFL record holder for most field goals in a season, earned his scholarship to Syracuse University in an unusual way: He and his father sent videotapes of Olindo kicking the ball at light posts on an empty field.

TRIVIA TIME
The Ravens' Matt Stover made field goals in 38 consecutive games from 1999 to 2001.
Whose record did he break?

A: Minnesota's Fred Cox (31 consecutive games from 1968 to 1970).

MOST FIELD GOALS, GAME

	PLAYER	TEAM	DATE	FGS
1	Jim Bakken	STC	9/24/67	7
=	Rich Karlis	MIN	11/5/89	7
=	Chris Boniol	DAL	11/18/96	7
4	Gino Cappelletti	BOS	10/4/64	6
=	Garo Yepremian	DET	11/13/66	6
=	Jim Turner	NYJ	11/3/68	6
=	Tom Dempsey	PHI	11/12/72	6
=	Bobby Howfield	NYJ	12/3/72	6
=	Jim Bakken	STC	12/9/73	6
=	Joe Danelo	NYG	10/18/81	6
=	Ray Wersching	SF	10/16/83	6
=	Gary Anderson*	PIT	10/23/88	6
=	John Carney*	SD	9/5/93	6
=	John Carney*	SD	9/19/93	6
=	Doug Pelfrey	CIN	11/6/94	6
=	Norm Johnson	ATL	11/13/94	6
=	Jeff Wilkins*	SF	9/29/96	6
=	Steve Christie*	BUF	10/20/96	6
=	Greg Davis	SD	10/5/97	6
=	Gary Anderson*	MIN	12/13/98	6
=	Olindo Mare*	MIA	10/17/99	6
=	Jason Hanson*	DET	10/17/99	6

LONGEST FIELD GOAL

	PLAYER	TEAM	DATE	YDS
1	Tom Dempsey	NO	11/8/70	63
=	Jason Elam*	DEN	10/25/98	63
3	Steve Cox	CLE	10/21/84	60
=	Morten Andersen*	NO	10/27/91	60
5	Tony Franklin	PHI	11/12/79	59
=	Pete Stoyanovich	MIA	11/12/89	59
=	Steve Christie*	BUF	9/26/93	59
=	Morten Andersen*	ATL	12/24/95	59
9	Dan Miller	BAC	12/26/82	58
=	Nick Lowery	KC	9/18/83	58
=	Steve Cox	CLE	12/4/83	58
=	Nick Lowery	KC	9/12/85	58

MOST FIELD GOALS MORE THAN 50 YARDS, SEASON

	PLAYER	TEAM	YEAR	FGS
1	Morten Andersen*	ATL	1995	8
2	Dean Biasucci	IND	1988	6
=	Chris Jacke	GB	1993	6
=	Tony Zendejas	RAM	1993	6
5	Fred Steinfort	DEN	1980	5
=	Norm Johnson	SEA	1986	5
=	Kevin Butler	CHI	1993	5
=	Jason Elam*	DEN	1995	5
=	Cary Blanchard	IND	1996	5
=	Jason Elam*	DEN	1999	5
=	Martín Gramática*	TB	2000	5

Morten Andersen's record-setting performance in 1995 included 3 field goals of more than 50 yards in a game against his former team, the New Orleans Saints.

BAREFOOT AND HAPPY

During the late 1970s and throughout the 1980s, a number of kickers plied their trade barefoot, claiming they made better contact with the ball. One of the most successful was Rich Karlis, who tied an NFL record by kicking 7 field goals in a 1989 game.

TIME OUT

OVERCOMING ADVERSITY

Though born with no right hand and only half of his right foot, Tom Dempsey prevailed over his physical limitations to become the New Orleans Saints' kicker in 1969. The next year, Dempsey kicked an NFL-record 63-yard field goal to give New Orleans a 19-17 victory over the Detroit Lions. Dempsey's kick shattered the previous record of 56 yards, set by the Baltimore Colts' Bert Rechichar in 1953.

HIGHEST FIELD GOAL PERCENTAGE, CAREER#

	PLAYER	FGS	ATT	PCT
1	Mike Vanderjagt*	114	130	87.7
2	Olindo Mare*	136	161	84.5
3	John Carney*	290	356	81.5
4	Matt Stover*	267	328	81.4
5	Ryan Longwell*	131	162	80.9
6	Mike Hollis*	175	217	80.6
7	Adam Vinatieri*	160	199	80.4
8	Doug Brien*	150	187	80.2
9	John Kasay*	231	288	80.2
10	Nick Lowery	383	479	80.0

#Minimum 100 attempts

Jan Stenerud, the first pure kicker elected to the Hall of Fame, made 68.8 percent of his attempts during his career (1967–1985).

MOST FIELD GOAL ATTEMPTS, CAREER

	PLAYER	ATT
1	George Blanda	641
2	Gary Anderson*	596
3	Morten Andersen*	590
4	Jan Stenerud	558
5	Jim Turner	490
6	Nick Lowery	479
7	Norm Johnson	477
8	Eddie Murray	466
9	Mark Moseley	457
10	Fred Cox	455

The Redskins' Mark Moseley is the only pure kicker to earn notice as the NFL's most valuable player (1982).

NEARLY PERFECT

Todd Peterson missed just one extra-point attempt in his first eight seasons. He failed to convert in week 8 of the 2001 season after making his first 219 extra-point kicks.

DID YOU KNOW?
Lou Groza, a member of the Pro Football Hall of Fame, led the NFL in field goals a record five times during his career. He's also the only player to lead the NFL in field goals for three consecutive seasons.

HIGHEST FIELD GOAL PERCENTAGE, SEASON

	PLAYER	TEAM	YEAR	FGS	FGA	PCT
1	Tony Zendejas	RAM	1991	17	17	100.0
=	Gary Anderson*	MIN	1998	35	35	100.0
=	Jeff Wilkins*	RAM	2000	17	17	100.0
4	Chris Boniol	DAL	1995	27	28	96.4
5	Norm Johnson	ATL	1993	26	27	96.3
=	Pete Stoyanovich*	KC	1997	26	27	96.3
7	Gary Anderson*	MIN	2000	22	23	95.7
8	Mark Moseley	WAS	1982	20	21	95.2
=	Eddie Murray	DET	1988	20	21	95.2
=	Eddie Murray	DET	1989	20	21	95.2

Mark Moseley, the NFL's last straight-ahead kicker, is the only player on this list who did not kick "soccer-style," i.e., approach from the side and kick with his instep.

MOST EXTRA POINTS, CAREER

	PLAYER	XPS
1	George Blanda	943
2	Gary Anderson*	705
3	Morten Andersen*	644
4	Lou Groza	641
5	Norm Johnson	638
6	Jan Stenerud	580
7	Nick Lowery	562
8	Pat Leahy	558
9	Al Del Greco	543
10	Eddie Murray	538

MOST FIELD GOAL ATTEMPTS, SEASON

	PLAYFR	TEAM	YEAR	ATT
1	Bruce Gossett	RAM	1966	49
=	Curt Knight	WAS	1971	49
3	Chester Marcol	GB	1972	48
4	Jim Turner	NYJ	1969	47
=	David Ray	RAM	1973	47
=	Mark Moseley	WAS	1983	47
7	Pete Gogolak	BUF	1965	46
=	Jim Turner	NYJ	1968	46
=	Fred Cox	MIN	1970	46
=	Olindo Mare*	MIA	1999	46

ALMOST A SURE THING

The Colts' Mike Vanderjagt rarely misses a field goal—his career accuracy rate of 87.7 percent (through 2001) is the best ever. From inside 50 yards, he misses even less— 104 field goals made in 114 attempts, a success rate of 91.2 percent.

LONG AND STRAIGHT

Jason Elam has displayed both power and accuracy during his NFL career. The power in Elam's leg was evident to all when he kicked an NFL record-tying 63-yard field goal just before halftime of a 1998 game against Jacksonville. The accuracy is reflected in the 344 consecutive extra-point attempts he has converted. That streak and his 99.7 extra-point percentage (368 of 369) are both NFL bests. Despite the fact that many of Elam's kicks occur in the inclement weather of the Rocky Mountains, he has not missed an extra-point attempt since his rookie season in 1993. The Broncos selected Elam in the third round of the 1993 NFL Draft out of Hawaii.

TIME OUT

*Active through 2001 season

PUNTERS

MOST PUNTS, GAME

	PLAYER	TEAM VS OPP	DATE	PUNTS
1	Leo Araguz*	OAK vs. SD	10/11/98	16
2	John Teltschik	PHI vs. NYG	12/6/87	15
3	Dick Nesbitt	CHC vs. CHI	11/30/33	14
=	Keith Molesworth	CHI vs. GB	12/10/33	14
=	Sammy Baugh	WAS vs. PHI	11/5/39	14
=	Carl Kinscherf	NYG vs. DET	11/7/43	14
=	George Taliaferro	NYY vs. RAM	9/28/51	14
8	Many tied with			13

HIGHEST AVERAGE YARDS PER PUNT, CAREER#

	PLAYER	PUNTS	YARDS	AVG
1	Sammy Baugh	338	15,245	45.1
2	Tommy Davis	511	22,833	44.7
3	Darren Bennett*	602	26,800	44.5
4	Yale Lary	503	22,279	44.3
5	Tom Rouen*	612	26,907	44.0
6	Bob Scarpitto	283	12,408	43.8
7	Horace Gillom	385	16,872	43.8
8	Jerry Norton	358	15,671	43.8
9	Dave Lewis	285	12,447	43.7
10	Todd Sauerbrun*	503	21,924	43.6

#Minimum 250 punts

HIGHEST AVERAGE YARDS PER PUNT, SEASON

	PLAYER	TEAM	YEAR	PUNTS	YARDS	AVG
1	Sammy Baugh	WAS	1940	35	1,799	51.4
2	Yale Lary	DET	1963	35	1,713	48.9
3	Sammy Baugh	WAS	1941	30	1,462	48.7
4	Yale Lary	DET	1961	52	2,519	48.4
5	Sammy Baugh	WAS	1942	37	1,785	48.2
6	Todd Sauerbrun*	CAR	2001	93	4,419	47.5
7	Joe Muha	PHI	1948	57	2,694	47.3
8	Craig Hentrich*	TEN	1998	69	3,258	47.2
9	George Gulyanics	CHI	1949	29	1,368	47.2
10	Yale Lary	DET	1959	45	2,121	47.1

ALL-AROUND TALENT

Not only did Pro Football Hall of Fame member Yale Lary have 3 of the top 10 single-season punting averages in NFL history, he also intercepted 50 passes, had 3 punt returns for touchdowns, and was selected to nine Pro Bowls.

DID YOU KNOW?
On September 21, 1969, Steve O'Neal of the New York Jets booted an NFL-record 98-yard punt in just the second game of his career.

MOST PUNTS, CAREER

PLAYER	PUNTS
1 Sean Landeta*	1,216
2 Lee Johnson*	1,212
3 Dave Jennings	1,154
4 Rohn Stark	1,141
5 Jeff Feagles*	1,139
6 John James	1,083
7 Jerrel Wilson	1,072
8 Brian Hansen	1,057
9 Ray Guy	1,049
10 Rich Camarillo	1,027

MOST PUNTS, SEASON

PLAYER	TEAM	YEAR	PUNTS
1 Bob Parsons	CHI	1981	114
2 Brad Maynard*	NYG	1997	111
3 John James	ATL	1978	109
4 John Teltschik	PHI	1986	108
= Rick Tuten	SEA	1992	108
= Chris Gardocki*	CLE	2000	108
7 Sean Landeta*	PHI	1999	107
8 David Beverly	GB	1978	106
= Chris Gardocki*	CLE	1999	106
10 Bob Scarpitto	DEN	1967	105
= John James	ATL	1977	105

QUICK KICK
Chris Gardocki, who has punted for the Bears, Colts, and Browns, has never had a punt blocked during his 11-year NFL career.

GOOD PUNTING, MATE

A former Australian Rules Football star, San Diego Chargers punter Darren Bennett has become a star in the NFL, too. Bennett, who was born and raised in Australia, came to the United States in 1994 after winning two round-trip airline tickets in a long-ball kicking contest. He and his wife journeyed to California for their honeymoon, and the 29-year-old Bennett convinced the Chargers to give him a tryout. San Diego signed him, and he has gone on to set numerous club records, earn two Pro Bowl berths, and be named the punter on the NFL's All-Decade Team.

TIME OUT

Active through 2001 season

HIGHEST AVERAGE KICKOFF RETURN, SEASON

	PLAYER	TEAM	YEAR	KRS	YARDS	AVG
1	Travis Williams	GB	1967	18	739	41.1
2	Gale Sayers	CHI	1967	16	603	37.7
3	Ollie Matson	CHC	1958	14	497	35.5
4	Jim Duncan	BAC	1970	20	707	35.4
5	Lynn Chandnois	PIT	1952	17	599	35.2
6	Preston Pearson	BAC	1968	15	527	35.1
7	Joe Arenas	SF	1953	16	551	34.4
8	Tom Watkins	DET	1965	17	584	34.4
9	Vitamin Smith	LA	1950	22	742	33.7
10	Bobby Williams	DET	1969	17	563	33.1

MOST KICKOFF RETURNS, SEASON

	PLAYER	TEAM	YEAR	KRS
1	MarTay Jenkins*	ARI	2000	82
2	Tyrone Hughes	NO	1996	70
3	Ronney Jenkins*	SD	2000	67
4	Tyrone Hughes	NO	1995	66
=	Charlie Rogers*	SEA	2000	66
6	Glyn Milburn*	DET	1996	64
7	Tyrone Hughes	NO	1994	63
=	Glyn Milburn*	CHI	2000	63
9	Andre Coleman	SD	1995	62
=	Glyn Milburn*	CHI	1998	62
=	Brock Marion*	MIA	1999	62

HIGHEST AVERAGE KICKOFF RETURN, CAREER#

	PLAYER	KRS	YARDS	AVG
1	Gale Sayers	91	2,781	30.6
2	Lynn Chandnois	92	2,720	29.6
3	Abe Woodson	193	5,538	28.7
4	Buddy Young	90	2,514	27.9
5	Travis Williams	102	2,801	27.5
6	Joe Arenas	139	3,798	27.3
7	Clarence Davis	79	2,140	27.1
8	Steve Van Buren	76	2,030	26.7
9	Lenny Lyles	81	2,161	26.7
10	Mercury Morris	111	2,947	26.5

#Minimum 75 returns

GOOD RATIO

Travis Williams's feat of 6 career kickoff returns for touchdowns is all the more remarkable considering he played just five seasons and returned just 102 career kickoffs.

RETURN ON INVESTMENT

On March 23, 1959, running back Ollie Matson made history by being traded by the Chicago Cardinals to the Los Angeles Rams for nine players. Matson had already etched his name in the NFL record book by virtue of his 6 kickoff returns for touchdowns. Matson's 6 scoring returns came during his first 86 kickoff returns. He added 3 touchdowns on punt returns to his résumé and went on to score 73 total touchdowns during his 15-year career (1952–1966). He was inducted into the Pro Football Hall of Fame in 1972.

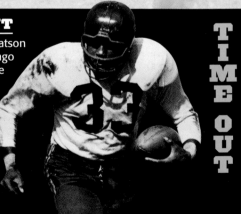

TIME OUT

DID YOU KNOW?

Only four players have returned two kickoffs for touchdowns in a game: Timmy Brown (PHI, 1966); Travis Williams (GB, 1967); Ron Brown (RAM, 1985); and Tyrone Hughes (NO, 1994).

MOST KICKOFF RETURN TOUCHDOWNS, CAREER

PLAYER	TDS
1 Mel Gray	6
= Ollie Matson	6
= Gale Sayers	6
= Travis Williams	6
5 Michael Bates*	5
= Timmy Brown	5
= Bobby Mitchell	5
= Abe Woodson	5
9 Seven tied with	4

When he led the league in kickoff return average in successive seasons (1996–97), the Panthers' Michael Bates became the first player to do so since Abe Woodson in 1962–63.

MOST KICKOFF RETURN TOUCHDOWNS, SEASON

PLAYER	TEAM	YEAR	TDS
1 Travis Williams	GB	1967	4
= Cecil Turner	CHI	1970	4
3 Vitamin Smith	RAM	1950	3
= Abe Woodson	SF	1963	3
= Gale Sayers	CHI	1967	3
= Raymond Clayborn	NE	1977	3
= Ron Brown	RAM	1985	3
= Mel Gray	DET	1994	3
= Darrick Vaughn	ATL	2000	3
10 Many players with			2

Four Pro Football Hall of Fame players have led the NFL in kickoff return average: Steve Van Buren, 1945; Ollie Matson, 1958; Gale Sayers, 1966; and Walter Payton, 1975. In addition, two future Hall of Fame members also have led the league in kickoff return average: Tim Brown, 1988; and Rod Woodson, 1989.

HE KEEPS GOING, AND GOING...
Brian Mitchell, who has played for the Redskins and Eagles, has more kickoff returns and more punt returns than any other player in NFL history.

MOST KICKOFF RETURNS, CAREER

PLAYER	KRS
1 Brian Mitchell*	509
2 Mel Gray	421
3 Glyn Milburn*	407
4 Michael Bates*	347
5 Desmond Howard*	333
6 Kevin R. Williams	322
7 Tyrone Hughes	283
8 Eric Metcalf*	278
9 Ron Smith	275
10 Dave Meggett	252

LONGEST KICKOFF RETURN

PLAYER	TEAM	DATE	YDS
1 Al Carmichael	GB	10/7/56	106
= Noland Smith	KC	12/17/67	106
= Roy Green	STC	10/21/79	106
4 Frank Seno	CHC	10/20/46	105
= Ollie Matson	CHC	10/14/56	105
= Abe Woodson	SF	11/8/59	105
= Timmy Brown	PHI	9/17/61	105
= Jon Arnett	RAM	10/29/61	105
= Eugene Morris	MIA	9/14/69	105
= Travis Williams	RAM	12/5/71	105
= Terry Fair	DET	9/28/98	105

Active through 2001 season

SPECIAL TEAMS

MOST PUNT RETURNS, CAREER

	PLAYER	PRS
1	Brian Mitchell*	388
2	Dave Meggett	349
3	Eric Metcalf*	348
4	Tim Brown*	310
5	Glyn Milburn*	304
6	Vai Sikahema	292
7	Billy Johnson	282
8	Darrien Gordon*	279
9	J.T. Smith	267
10	Emlen Tunnell	262

MOST PUNT RETURNS, SEASON

	PLAYER	TEAM	YEAR	PRS
1	Danny Reece	TB	1979	70
2	Fulton Walker	RAI	1985	62
3	J.T. Smith	KC	1979	58
=	Greg Pruitt	RAI	1983	58
=	Leo Lewis	MIN	1988	58
=	Desmond Howard*	GB	1996	58
7	Eddie Brown	WAS	1977	57
=	Danny Reece	TB	1980	57
=	Jeff Fisher	CHI	1984	57
=	Lew Barnes	CHI	1986	57
=	Jermaine Lewis*	BAL	1999	57

MOST PUNT RETURN TOUCHDOWNS, CAREER

	PLAYER	TDS
1	Eric Metcalf*	10
2	Jack Christiansen	8
=	Desmond Howard*	8
=	Brian Mitchell*	8
=	Rick Upchurch	8
6	Dave Meggett	7
7	Darrien Gordon*	6
=	Billy Johnson	6
=	Jermaine Lewis*	6
=	Deion Sanders	6

MOST PUNT RETURN TOUCHDOWNS, SEASON

	PLAYER	TEAM	YEAR	TDS
1	Jack Christiansen	DET	1951	4
=	Rick Upchurch	DEN	1976	4
3	Emlen Tunnell	NYG	1951	3
=	Billy Johnson	HOU	1975	3
=	LeRoy Irvin	RAM	1981	3
=	Desmond Howard*	GB	1996	3
=	Darrien Gordon*	DEN	1997	3
=	Eric Metcalf*	SD	1997	3
9	Many players with			2

OFF AND RUNNING
As a rookie in 1951, future Pro Football Hall of Fame defensive back Jack Christiansen scored on 4 of his 18 punt returns.

DID YOU KNOW?
In 2001, the Patriots' Troy Brown became the first player in NFL history to have at least 100 receptions (101) and lead the league in punt-return average (14.2) in the same season.

Wilson
NFL

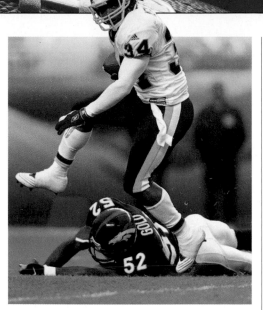

HIGHEST AVERAGE PUNT RETURN, CAREER[#]

	PLAYER	PRS	YARDS	AVG
1	George McAfee	112	1,431	12.78
2	Jack Christiansen	85	1,084	12.75
3	Claude Gibson	110	1,381	12.55
4	Darrien Gordon*	279	3,421	12.26
5	Bill Dudley	124	1,515	12.22
6	Rick Upchurch	248	3,008	12.13
7	Desmond Howard*	235	2,847	12.11
8	Jermaine Lewis*	231	2,730	11.82
9	Billy Johnson	282	3,317	11.76
10	Mack Herron	84	982	11.69

[#]Minimum 75 returns

WHO NEEDS PRACTICE?

After being out of football for a year and a half, Eric Metcalf returned a punt 89 yards for a touchdown the first time he touched the ball for the Redskins during the 2001 season.

MOST PUNT RETURNS, GAME

	PLAYER	TEAM	DATE	PRS
1	Eddie Brown	WAS	10/9/77	11
2	Theo Bell	PIT	12/16/79	10
=	Mike Nelms	WAS	12/26/82	10
=	Ronnie Harris	NE	12/5/93	10
5	Rodger Bird	OAK	9/10/67	9
=	Ralph McGill	SF	10/29/72	9
=	Ed Podolak	KC	11/10/74	9
=	Anthony Leonard	SF	10/17/76	9
=	Butch Johnson	DAL	11/15/76	9
=	Larry Marshall	PHI	9/18/77	9
=	Nesby Glasgow	BAC	9/2/79	9
=	Mike Nelms	WAS	12/21/80	9
=	Leon Bright	NYG	12/11/82	9
=	Pete Shaw	NYG	11/20/83	9
=	Cleotha Montgomery	RAI	12/10/84	9
=	Phil McConkey	NYG	12/6/87	9
=	Andre Hastings	PIT	11/13/95	9

HIGHEST AVERAGE PUNT RETURN, SEASON

	PLAYER	TEAM	YEAR	PRS	YDS	AVG
1	Herb Rich	BAC	1950	12	276	23.0
2	Jack Christiansen	DET	1952	15	322	21.5
3	Dick Christy	NYT	1961	18	383	21.3
4	Red Cochran	CHC	1949	15	314	20.9
5	Jerry Davis	CHC	1948	16	334	20.9
6	Bob Hayes	DAL	1968	15	312	20.8
7	Buddy Young	NYY	1951	12	231	19.3
8	Billy Grimes	GB	1950	29	555	19.1
9	Jack Christiansen	DET	1951	18	343	19.1
10	Ollie Matson	CHC	1955	13	245	18.8

HE NEVER DID IT AGAIN

Minnesota Vikings rookie Charlie West tied a then-NFL record by returning a punt 98 yards for a touchdown in a 1968 game. West's teammates were thrilled, but coach Bud Grant was not happy. Grant never wanted his players to field the punt inside the 10-yard line. As West was being congratulated by teammates, Grant called him over and said, "Charlie, if you ever do that again, you'll never play another down for the Minnesota Vikings." West kept his job, but the touchdown turned out to be the only one of his 12-year career.

TIME OUT

Active through 2001 season

DEFENSE

OPPONENTS' FUMBLES RECOVERED, CAREER

	PLAYER	FRS
1	Jim Marshall	29
2	Rickey Jackson	28
3	Cornelius Bennett	26
=	Kevin Greene	26
5	Dick Butkus	25
6	Chris Doleman	24
=	James Hasty	24
8	Carl Eller	23
=	Reggie Williams	23
10	Joe Fortunato	22
=	Sam Mills	22
=	Alan Page	22
=	Andy Robustelli	22

OPPONENTS' FUMBLES RECOVERED, SEASON

	PLAYER	TEAM	YEAR	FRS
1	Don Hultz	MIN	1963	9
2	Joe Schmidt	DET	1955	8
3	Alan Page	MIN	1970	7
=	Jack Lambert	PIT	1976	7
=	Ray Childress	HOU	1988	7
=	Rickey Jackson	NO	1990	7
7	Many tied with			6

NFL NOTEBOOK
Jack Tatum and Aeneas Williams share the NFL record for longest fumble return (104 yards). Tatum's return in September, 1972 helped the Oakland Raiders defeat the Green Bay Packers 20-14.

STUNNING START
Aeneas Williams's 104-yard fumble return for a touchdown in the opening minutes of a November, 2000 game helped the Arizona Cardinals upset the Washington Redskins.

DID YOU KNOW?
On November 28, 1948, Fred (Dippy) Evans of the Chicago Bears became the only player in NFL history to return 2 fumbles for touchdowns in a game.

RICKEY, YOU'RE SO FINE
Rickey Jackson, who recovered 28 career opponent fumbles, was a six-time Pro Bowl selection during his 15-year career.

MOST FUMBLES, GAME

	PLAYER	TEAM	DATE	FMBS
1	Len Dawson	KC	11/15/64	7
2	Sam Etcheverry	STC	9/17/61	6
=	Dave Krieg	SEA	11/5/89	6
=	Brett Favre*	GB	12/7/98	6
5	Paul Christman	CHC	11/10/46	5
=	Charlie Conerly	NYG	12/1/57	5
=	Jack Kemp	BUF	10/29/67	5
=	Roman Gabriel	PHI	11/21/76	5
=	R. Cunningham*	PHI	11/30/86	5
=	Willie Totten	BUF	10/4/87	5
=	Dave Walter	CIN	10/11/87	5
=	Dave Krieg	SEA	11/25/90	5
=	Andre Ware	DET	12/6/92	5
=	Steve Beuerlein*	CAR	11/8/98	5

MOST FUMBLES, SEASON

	PLAYER	TEAM	YEAR	FMBS
1	Kerry Collins*	NYG	2001	23
2	Tony Banks*	RAM	1996	21
3	Dave Krieg	SEA	1989	18
=	Warren Moon	HOU	1990	18
5	Dan Pastorini	HOU	1973	17
=	Warren Moon	HOU	1984	17
=	R. Cunningham*	PHI	1989	17
=	Jon Kitna*	SEA	2000	17
9	Many tied with			16

MOST FUMBLES, CAREER

	PLAYER	FUMBLES
1	Warren Moon	161
2	Dave Krieg	153
3	John Elway	137
4	Boomer Esiason	123
5	Dan Marino	110
6	Dan Fouts	106
7	Randall Cunningham*	105
=	Roman Gabriel	105
9	Brett Favre*	101
10	Vinny Testaverde*	95
=	Johnny Unitas	95

OVERLOOKED

TIME OUT

Despite being the all-time leading tackler at Valdosta State, Jessie Tuggle was not drafted by an NFL team. Undaunted, he signed with the Atlanta Falcons and made the club in 1987. Tuggle led the Falcons in tackles for nine consecutive seasons (1989–1997), and returned an NFL-record 5 of his 10 fumble recoveries for touchdowns.

*Active through 2001 season

MOST SEASONS PLAYED

	PLAYER	SEASONS
1	George Blanda	26
2	Earl Morrall	21
3	Morten Andersen*	20
=	Gary Anderson*	20
=	Jim Marshall	20
=	Jackie Slater	20
7	Many tied with	19

George Blanda played in four different decades during his 26-year career (1949–1958, 1960–1975).

MOST SEASONS WITH ONE CLUB

	PLAYER	TEAM	SEASONS
1	Jackie Slater	RAM	20
2	Darrell Green*	WAS	19
=	Jim Marshall	MIN	19
=	Bruce Matthews*	TEN	19
5	Jim Hart	STC	18
=	Pat Leahy	NYJ	18
=	Jeff Van Note	ATL	18

When Bruce Matthews started his career in 1983, he played for the Houston Oilers, who moved to Tennessee in 1997 and later were renamed the Titans.

NFL NOTEBOOK

Most of Earl Morrall's 21 seasons were spent as a backup quarterback, but he nevertheless played a pivotal role in NFL history. He won the 1968 NFL MVP award, led the Colts to victory in Super Bowl V, and guided the Dolphins to 10 victories in 1972 during their 17-0 year, the only perfect season in NFL history.

STILL KICKIN'

George Blanda received national acclaim in 1970, when the 43-year-old quarterback's last-minute heroics propelled the Raiders to four victories and a tie during a five-game stretch.

DID YOU KNOW?
During a 17-year span, from 1962–1978, Minnesota Vikings teammates Jim Marshall and Mick Tingelhoff never missed a Vikings' game—an astounding 240 consecutive games.

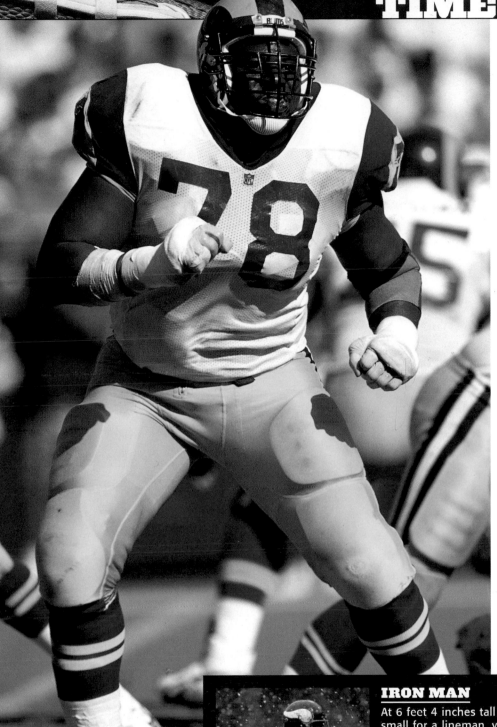

MOST GAMES PLAYED, CAREER

	PLAYER	GMS
1	George Blanda	340
2	Gary Anderson*	309
3	Morten Andersen*	308
4	Bruce Matthews*	296
5	Jim Marshall	282
6	Trey Junkin*	281
7	Darrell Green*	279
8	Clay Matthews	278
9	Norm Johnson	273
10	Jan Stenerud	263

MOST CONSECUTIVE GAMES PLAYED

	PLAYER	GMS
1	Jim Marshall	282
2	Mick Tingelhoff	240
3	Jim Bakken	234
=	Morten Andersen*	234
=	Gary Anderson*	234
6	Bruce Matthews*	232
7	George Blanda	224
=	Jeff Feagles*	224
=	Bill Romanowski*	224
10	Clyde Simmons	218

CORNERSTONE

Jackie Slater's 20 years with the Rams helped vault him into the Pro Football Hall of Fame.

IRON MAN

At 6 feet 4 inches tall and 248 pounds, Jim Marshall was small for a lineman, yet the Vikings' defensive end never missed a game in 20 seasons—an amazing run of 282 consecutive contests (plus another 21 games in the playoffs). Twice he had to leave hospitals (fighting pneumonia and ulcers) to continue his streak, and he excelled throughout his career despite regularly facing off against much larger players. Marshall, who began his career in Cleveland (1960), joined the Vikings in 1961 and spent the next 19 seasons as part of Minnesota's famed "Purple People Eaters" defense.

TIME OUT

* Active through 2001 season

MOST SACKS, ACTIVE PLAYERS

	PLAYER	YEARS	SACKS
1	Bruce Smith*	17	186.0
2	John Randle*	12	125.0
3	Trace Armstrong*	13	99.0
4	Robert Porcher*	10	85.5
5	Michael Strahan*	9	84.0
6	Michael Sinclair*	10	73.5
7	Michael McCrary*	9	69.0
8	Rob Burnett*	12	67.0
9	Kevin Carter*	7	64.5
=	Warren Sapp*	7	64.5

NFL NOTEBOOK

Aeneas Williams, who ranks fourth among active players with 50 career interceptions, set an NFL postseason record by returning 2 interceptions for scores to help the Rams defeat the Packers in a 2001 playoff game.

SACK MASTER

John Randle, now with the Seahawks, recorded eight consecutive seasons (1992–99) with double-digit sack totals for the Vikings.

HIGHEST PASSER RATING, ACTIVE QUARTERBACKS[#]

	PLAYER	YEARS	COMP PCT	YDS	TDS	INT	RATING
1	Kurt Warner*	4	66.9	12,651	98	53	103.0
2	Jeff Garcia*	3	62.2	10,360	74	33	91.5
3	Brett Favre*	11	60.8	38,627	287	172	86.8
4	Peyton Manning*	4	61.0	16,418	111	81	85.1
5	Mark Brunell*	8	60.3	22,521	125	79	85.0
6	Brian Griese*	4	60.6	8,549	56	38	83.6
7	Brad Johnson*	8	61.6	16,379	92	68	83.1
8	Rich Gannon*	13	59.2	22,256	145	88	83.1
9	Neil O'Donnell*	11	57.7	21,434	118	67	81.7
10	Randall Cunningham*	16	56.6	29,979	207	134	81.5

[#]Minimum 1,000 pass attempts

MOST INTERCEPTIONS, ACTIVE PLAYERS

	PLAYER	YEARS	INT
1	Rod Woodson*	15	61
2	Eric Allen*	14	54
=	Darrell Green*	19	54
4	Aeneas Williams*	11	50
5	Ray Buchanan*	9	43
6	Terrell Buckley*	10	41
7	LeRoy Butler*	12	38
8	Troy Vincent*	10	37
=	Eric Davis*	12	37
10	Todd Lyght*	11	35

DID YOU KNOW?
The all-time records for rushing yards and sacks may be broken in 2002. Emmitt Smith is 539 yards shy of the rushing mark, and Bruce Smith is 12 sacks shy of the sacks record.

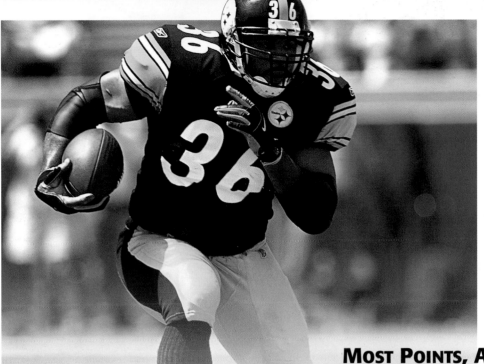

THE BUS ROLLS ON

Jerome Bettis rushed for 1,000 or more yards in eight of his first nine seasons.

MOST RECEPTIONS, ACTIVE PLAYERS

PLAYER	YEARS	REC
1 Jerry Rice*	16	1,364
2 Cris Carter*	14	1,093
3 Tim Brown*	14	937
4 Larry Centers*	12	765
5 Shannon Sharpe*	12	692
6 Herman Moore*	11	670
7 Terance Mathis*	12	666
8 Rob Moore*	12	628
9 Tony Martin*	12	593
10 Jimmy Smith*	8	584

Smith's 562 receptions the past six seasons are the most in the NFL during that span.

MOST POINTS, ACTIVE PLAYERS

PLAYER	YEARS	TDS	FGS	XPS#	TOTAL
1 Gary Anderson*	20	0	476	705	2,133
2 Morten Andersen*	20	0	464	644	2,036
3 Steve Christie*	12	0	281	364	1,207
4 John Carney*	14	0	290	331	1,201
5 Jerry Rice*	17	196	0	(4)	1,184
6 Matt Stover*	11	0	267	333	1,134
7 Jason Elam*	9	0	235	368	1,073
8 Jason Hanson*	10	0	239	327	1,044
9 John Kasay*	11	0	231	271	964
10 Emmitt Smith*	12	159	0	(1)	956

#Numbers in parentheses denote 2-point conversions scored.

MOST RUSHING YARDS, ACTIVE PLAYERS

PLAYER	YEARS	YARDS
1 Emmitt Smith*	12	16,187
2 Jerome Bettis*	9	10,876
3 Ricky Watters*	10	10,643
4 Marshall Faulk*	8	9,442
5 Curtis Martin*	7	9,267
6 Terry Allen*	10	8,614
7 Eddie George*	6	7,813
8 Terrell Davis*	7	7,607
9 Corey Dillon*	5	6,209
10 Garrison Hearst*	9	6,145

APPROACHING 1,000

Raiders receiver Tim Brown entered the 2002 season on pace to become the third player in NFL history to surpass 1,000 career receptions. (The first 1,000-catch player was Jerry Rice, now Brown's teammate.) Brown, who won the 1987 Heisman Trophy while playing for Notre Dame, joined the Raiders as a first-round pick in 1988. A knee injury slowed him early in his career, but he rebounded to record nine consecutive seasons (1993–2001) with 1,000 or more receiving yards and earn a spot among the NFL's all-time greats.

TIME OUT

* Active through 2001 season

ALL-PURPOSE YARDS

MOST ALL-PURPOSE YARDS, CAREER

PLAYER	RUSH	REC	PR	KR	FMBS	TOTAL
1 Walter Payton	16,726	4,538	0	539	0	21,803
2 Jerry Rice*	625	20,386	0	6	0	21,017
3 Brian Mitchell	1,947	2,298	4,278	11,735	5	20,263
4 Emmitt Smith*	16,187	2,923	0	0	0	19,110
5 Barry Sanders	15,269	2,921	0	118	0	18,308
6 Herschel Walker	8,225	4,859	0	5,084	0	18,168
7 Tim Brown*	171	13,237	3,217	1,235	3	17,863
8 Marcus Allen	12,243	5,411	0	0	-6	17,648
9 Eric Metcalf*	2,385	5,572	3,454	5,772	0	17,183
10 Thurman Thomas	12,074	4,458	0	0	0	16,532

MOST ALL-PURPOSE YARDS, SEASON

PLAYER	TEAM	YEAR	RUSH	REC	PR	KR	TOTAL
1 Derrick Mason*	TEN	2000	1	895	662	1,132	2,690
2 Lionel James	SD	1985	516	1,027	213	779	2,535
3 Brian Mitchell*	WAS	1994	311	236	452	1,478	2,477
4 Terry Metcalf	STC	1975	816	378	285	960	2,462
5 Mack Herron	NE	1974	824	474	517	629	2,444
6 Gale Sayers	CHI	1966	1,231	447	44	718	2,440
7 Marshall Faulk*	RAM	1999	1,381	1,048	0	0	2,429
8 Timmy Brown	PHI	1963	841	487	152	945	2,428
9 MarTay Jenkins*	ARI	2000	-4	219	1	2,186	2,402
10 Barry Sanders	DET	1997	2,053	305	0	0	2,358

Terry Metcalf's total includes 23 fumble-return yards and Timmy Brown's total includes 3 fumble-return yards, which aren't included on this list.

VALUABLE PERFORMER

Tennessee's versatile Derrick Mason tallied 2,690 all-purpose yards in 2000, shattering Lionel James's 15-year-old NFL record.

NFL NOTEBOOK

Marshall Faulk is the only player to post four consecutive seasons (1998–2001) with at least 2,000 yards from scrimmage, breaking Walter Payton's record of three consecutive seasons (1983–85).

MOST YARDS FROM SCRIMMAGE, CAREER

PLAYER	YRS	YARDS
1 Walter Payton	13	21,264
2 Jerry Rice*	17	21,011
3 Emmitt Smith*	12	19,110
4 Barry Sanders	10	18,190
5 Marcus Allen	16	17,654
6 Thurman Thomas	13	16,532
7 Tony Dorsett	12	16,293
8 Eric Dickerson	11	15,396
9 Ricky Watters*	10	14,891
10 Marshall Faulk*	8	14,889

DID YOU KNOW?

The top three rookie record holders for most all-purpose yards are Tim Brown, Gale Sayers, and Eric Dickerson. Sayers and Dickerson are in the Pro Football Hall of Fame, and Brown will be soon.

MOST YARDS FROM SCRIMMAGE, SEASON

	PLAYER	TEAM	YEAR	YDS
1	Marshall Faulk*	RAM	1999	2,429
2	Barry Sanders	DET	1997	2,358
3	Marcus Allen	RAI	1985	2,314
4	Edgerrin James*	IND	2000	2,303
5	Eric Dickerson	RAM	1984	2,244
6	O.J. Simpson	BUF	1975	2,243
7	James Wilder	TB	1984	2,229
8	Marshall Faulk*	IND	1998	2,227
9	Terrell Davis*	DEN	1998	2,225
10	Eric Dickerson	RAM	1983	2,212

MOST YARDS FROM SCRIMMAGE, ROOKIE SEASON

	PLAYER	TEAM	YEAR	YDS
1	Eric Dickerson	RAM	1983	2,212
2	Edgerrin James*	IND	1999	2,139
3	Billy Sims	DET	1980	1,924
4	Ottis Anderson	STC	1979	1,913
5	Marshall Faulk*	IND	1994	1,804
6	George Rogers	NO	1981	1,800
7	Curt Warner	SEA	1983	1,774
8	Barry Sanders	DET	1989	1,752
9	Curtis Martin*	NE	1995	1,748
10	Jamal Lewis*	BAL	2000	1,660

BEFORE BARRY SANDERS...
The number 20 has been a lucky one for the Detroit Lions. Billy Sims donned that jersey when he joined the club in 1980 and went on to run for 3,812 total yards and score 31 touchdowns in his first two seasons before a knee injury curtailed his career.

LIVIN' UP TO THE HYPE

Great expectations greeted University of South Carolina running back George Rogers when he entered the NFL after winning the 1980 Heisman Trophy and being the first pick of the 1981 NFL Draft. The New Orleans Saints' rookie did not disappoint, leading the league in attempts (378) and rushing yards (1,674, a record for rookies at the time) while scoring 13 touchdowns. Rogers posted three additional 1,000-yard seasons and scored 18 touchdowns for the Redskins in 1986 before injuries led to his retirement following the 1987 season.

TIME OUT

Active through 2001 season

TOP 10 SUPER BOWL

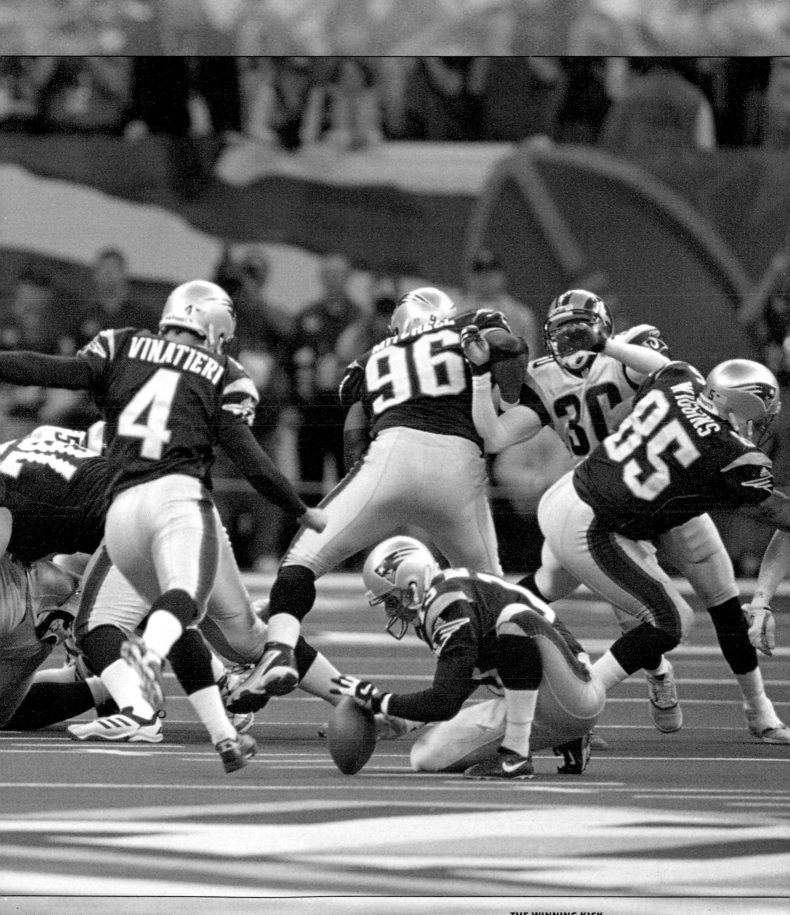

THE WINNING KICK

In Super Bowl XXXVI, Adam Vinatieri lived every kicker's dream—his 48-yard field goal as time expired gave the New England Patriots a 20-17 victory over the St. Louis Rams.

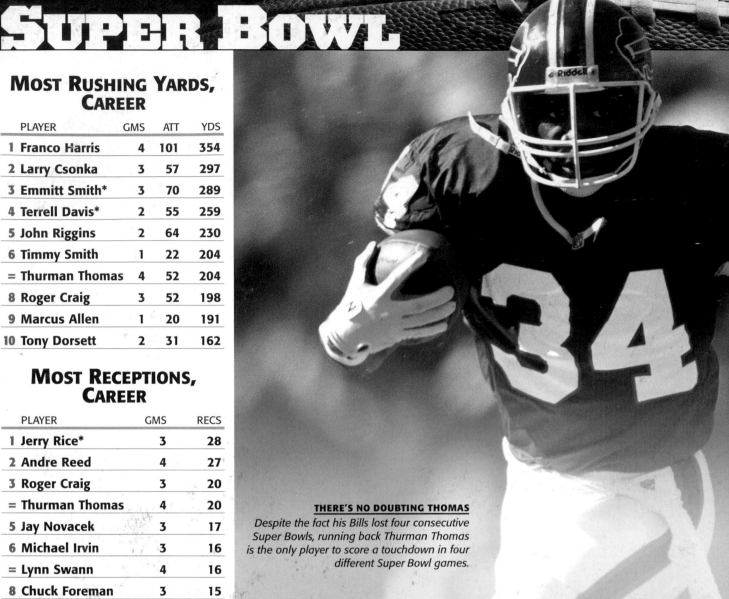

MOST RUSHING YARDS, CAREER

	PLAYER	GMS	ATT	YDS
1	Franco Harris	4	101	354
2	Larry Csonka	3	57	297
3	Emmitt Smith*	3	70	289
4	Terrell Davis*	2	55	259
5	John Riggins	2	64	230
6	Timmy Smith	1	22	204
=	Thurman Thomas	4	52	204
8	Roger Craig	3	52	198
9	Marcus Allen	1	20	191
10	Tony Dorsett	2	31	162

MOST RECEPTIONS, CAREER

	PLAYER	GMS	RECS
1	Jerry Rice*	3	28
2	Andre Reed	4	27
3	Roger Craig	3	20
=	Thurman Thomas	4	20
5	Jay Novacek	3	17
6	Michael Irvin	3	16
=	Lynn Swann	4	16
8	Chuck Foreman	3	15
9	Cliff Branch	3	14
10	Don Beebe	4	12
=	Kenneth Davis	4	12
=	Antonio Freeman*	2	12
=	Torry Holt*	2	12
=	Preston Pearson	5	12

THERE'S NO DOUBTING THOMAS

Despite the fact his Bills lost four consecutive Super Bowls, running back Thurman Thomas is the only player to score a touchdown in four different Super Bowl games.

NFL NOTEBOOK

Only 2 of the 7 kickoff returns for touchdowns in the Super Bowl have contributed to a victory. The Packers' Desmond Howard had a 99-yard kickoff return for a touchdown in Super Bowl XXXI, and the Ravens' Jermaine Lewis had an 84-yard kickoff return in Super Bowl XXXV.

HIGHEST PASSER RATING, CAREER#

	PLAYER	GMS	ATT	COMP	PCT	YDS	TDS	INT	RATING
1	Joe Montana	4	122	83	68.0	1,142	11	0	127.8
2	Jim Plunkett	2	46	29	63.0	433	4	0	122.8
3	Terry Bradshaw	4	84	49	58.3	932	9	4	112.8
4	Troy Aikman	3	80	56	70.0	689	5	1	111.9
5	Bart Starr	2	47	29	61.7	452	3	1	106.0
6	Brett Favre*	2	69	39	56.5	502	5	1	97.6
7	Roger Staubach	4	98	61	62.2	734	8	4	95.4
8	Kurt Warner*	2	89	52	58.4	779	3	2	89.1
9	Len Dawson	2	44	28	63.6	353	2	2	84.8
10	Bob Griese	3	41	26	63.4	295	1	2	72.7

#Minimum 40 pass attempts

DID YOU KNOW?
Twelve players have played in five or more Super Bowl games, but only Charles Haley has five Super Bowl rings. His teams were victorious in games XXIII, XXIV, XXVII, XXVIII, and XXX.

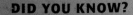

MOST GAMES, CAREER

	PLAYER	TEAM(S)	GMS
1	Mike Lodish	BUF/DEN	6
2	Marv Fleming	GB/MIA	5
=	Larry Cole	DAL	5
=	Cliff Harris	DAL	5
=	Charles Haley	SF/DAL	5
=	D.D. Lewis	DAL	5
=	Preston Pearson	BAC/PIT/DAL	5
=	Charlie Waters	DAL	5
=	Rayfield Wright	DAL	5
=	Cornelius Bennett	BUF/ATL	5
=	John Elway	DEN	5
=	Glenn Parker*	BUF/NYG	5

SIX SUPER BOWL SHARES

Mike Lodish is the only player in NFL history to play in six Super Bowls. He was able to taste victory in his last two appearances with the Broncos in Super Bowls XXXII and XXXIII.

MOST TOUCHDOWNS, CAREER

	PLAYER	GMS	TDS
1	Jerry Rice*	3	7
2	Emmitt Smith*	3	5
3	Roger Craig	3	4
=	John Elway	5	4
=	Franco Harris	4	4
=	Thurman Thomas	4	4
7	Cliff Branch	3	3
=	Terrell Davis*	2	3
=	Antonio Freeman*	2	3
=	John Stallworth	4	3
=	Lynn Swann	4	3
=	Ricky Watters*	1	3

MOST RECEIVING YARDS, CAREER

	PLAYER	GMS	RECS	YDS
1	Jerry Rice*	3	28	512
2	Lynn Swann	4	16	364
3	Andre Reed	4	27	323
4	John Stallworth	4	11	268
5	Michael Irvin	3	16	256
6	Ricky Sanders	2	10	234
7	Antonio Freeman*	2	12	231
8	Isaac Bruce*	2	11	218
9	Roger Craig	3	20	212
10	Cliff Branch	3	14	181

Lynn Swann's career record of 364 receiving yards, set during the 1970s, lasted more than a decade until Jerry Rice surpassed him in Super Bowl XXIX, played in January 1995.

Active through 2001 season

SUPER BOWL

MOST TOUCHDOWNS, GAME

	PLAYER	TEAM	GAME	TDS
1	Roger Craig	SF	XXIII	3
=	Jerry Rice*	SF	XXIV	3
=	Jerry Rice*	SF	XXIX	3
=	Ricky Watters*	SF	XXIX	3
=	Terrell Davis*	DEN	XXXII	3
6	26 players with 2. Most recent:			
=	Emmitt Smith*	DAL	XXVII	2
=	Emmitt Smith*	DAL	XXVIII	2
=	Antonio Freeman*	GB	XXXI	2
=	Howard Griffith	DEN	XXXIII	2
=	Eddie George*	TEN	XXXIV	2

Terrell Davis is the only player to rush for 3 touchdowns in a Super Bowl.

MOST RUSHING YARDS, GAME

	PLAYER	TEAM	GAME	YDS
1	Timmy Smith	WAS	XXII	204
2	Marcus Allen	RAI	XVIII	191
3	John Riggins	WAS	XVII	166
4	Franco Harris	PIT	IX	158
5	Terrell Davis*	DEN	XXXII	157
6	Larry Csonka	MIA	VIII	145
7	Clarence Davis	OAK	XI	137
8	Thurman Thomas	BUF	XXV	135
9	Emmitt Smith	DAL	XXVIII	132
10	Matt Snell	NYJ	III	121

GAMEBREAKER

Marcus Allen's cutback 74-yard touchdown run in Super Bowl XVIII remains the only rushing play of more than 60 yards in Super Bowl history.

TRIVIA TIME
Of the top 10 single-game Super Bowl rushing totals, only one runner played for a losing team. Can you name him?

A: Thurman Thomas for Buffalo in XXV.

BIG GAME DAN

Tight end Dan Ross had 11 receptions for the Bengals in Super Bowl XVI—more catches than he had in any other game of his career.

MOST RECEPTIONS, GAME

	PLAYER	TEAM	GAME	REC
1	Dan Ross	CIN	XVI	11
=	Jerry Rice*	SF	XXIII	11
3	Tony Nathan	MIA	XIX	10
=	Jerry Rice*	SF	XXIX	10
=	Andre Hastings	PIT	XXX	10
6	Ricky Sanders	WAS	XXII	9
=	Antonio Freeman*	GB	XXXII	9
8	George Sauer	NYJ	III	8
=	Roger Craig	SF	XXIII	8
=	Andre Reed	BUF	XXV	8
=	Andre Reed	BUF	XXVII	8
=	Ronnie Harmon	SD	XXIX	8

Jerry Rice is the only player on this list to win the Super Bowl MVP award, for XXIII.

* Active through 2001 season

MOST PASSING YARDS, GAME

	PLAYER	TEAM	GAME	YDS
1	Kurt Warner*	RAM	XXXIV	414
2	Kurt Warner*	RAM	XXXVI	365
3	Joe Montana	SF	XXIII	357
4	Doug Williams	WAS	XXII	340
5	John Elway	DEN	XXXIII	336
6	Joe Montana	SF	XIX	331
7	Steve Young	SF	XXIX	325
8	Terry Bradshaw	PIT	XIII	318
=	Dan Marino	MIA	XIX	318
10	Terry Bradshaw	PIT	XIV	309

MOST RECEIVING YARDS, GAME

	PLAYER	TEAM	GAME	YDS
1	Jerry Rice*	SF	XXIII	215
2	Ricky Sanders	WAS	XXII	193
3	Isaac Bruce*	RAM	XXXIV	162
4	Lynn Swann	PIT	X	161
5	Andre Reed	BUF	XXVII	152
=	Rod Smith*	DEN	XXXIII	152
7	Jerry Rice*	SF	XXIX	149
8	Jerry Rice*	SF	XXIV	148
9	Max McGee	GB	I	138
10	George Sauer	NYJ	III	133

LONGEST PLAY FROM SCRIMMAGE#

	PLAYERS	TEAM	GAME	PASS/RUN	YDS
1	Brett Favre* to Antonio Freeman*	GB	XXXI	Pass	81
2	Jim Plunkett to Kenny King	OAK	XV	Pass	80
=	Doug Williams to Ricky Sanders	WAS	XXII	Pass	80
=	John Elway to Rod Smith*	DEN	XXXIII	Pass	80
5	David Woodley to Jimmy Cefalo	MIA	XVII	Pass	76
6	Johnny Unitas to John Mackey	BAC	V	Pass	75
=	Terry Bradshaw to John Stallworth	PIT	XIII	Pass	75
8	Marcus Allen	RAI	XVIII	Run	74
9	Terry Bradshaw to John Stallworth	PIT	XIV	Pass	73
=	Kurt Warner* to Isaac Bruce*	RAM	XXXIV	Pass	73

#All of the plays resulted in touchdowns.

ONE SPECIAL GAME

Rookie Timmy Smith had just 29 regular-season carries entering the 1987 postseason. Smith began to establish himself in the playoffs and earned the starting assignment for Super Bowl XXII. Smith proceeded to rush for a Super Bowl record 204 yards (on just 22 carries) and 2 touchdowns in Washington's 42-10 victory. He rushed for 122 yards, including a 58-yard scoring jaunt, in Washington's memorable 35-point second quarter. He played only 15 more NFL games before injuries and off-field problems derailed his career.

TIME OUT

SUPER BOWL

MOST COMPLETIONS, GAME

PLAYER	GAME	COMP
1 Jim Kelly	XXVIII	31
2 Dan Marino	XIX	29
3 Jim Kelly	XXVI	28
= Neil O'Donnell*	XXX	28
= Kurt Warner*	XXXVI	28
6 Ken Anderson	XVI	25
= Drew Bledsoe*	XXXI	25
= Brett Favre*	XXXII	25
9 Joe Montana	XIX	24
= Stan Humphries	XXIX	24
= Steve Young	XXIX	24
= Kurt Warner*	XXXIV	24

None of the quarterbacks who completed 25 or more passes were victorious in those games.

MOST PASSING TOUCHDOWNS, GAME

PLAYER	GAME	TDS
1 Steve Young	XXIX	6
2 Joe Montana	XXIV	5
3 Terry Bradshaw	XIII	4
= Doug Williams	XXII	4
= Troy Aikman	XXVII	4
6 Roger Staubach	XIII	3
= Jim Plunkett	XV	3
= Joe Montana	XIX	3
= Phil Simms	XXI	3
= Brett Favre•	XXXII	3

Steve Young's 6 touchdown passes are the most ever in a postseason game, tied with Oakland's Daryle Lamonica, who had 6 against Houston in a 1969 playoff game.

BUFFALO'S MAIN MAN
Jim Kelly holds Super Bowl records for most completions in a game (31 against Dallas in XXVIII) and most attempts in a game (58 against Washington in XXVI).

HIGHEST COMPLETION PERCENTAGE, GAME

PLAYER	GAME	COMP	ATT	PCT
1 Phil Simms	XXI	22	25	88.0
2 Joe Montana	XXIV	22	29	75.9
3 Ken Anderson	XVI	25	34	73.5
4 Troy Aikman	XXVII	22	30	73.3
5 Troy Aikman	XXVIII	19	27	70.3
6 Bart Starr	I	16	23	69.6
7 Joe Montana	XIX	24	35	68.6
8 Roger Staubach	XII	17	25	68.0
9 Terry Bradshaw	XIV	14	21	66.7
10 Steve Young	XXIX	24	36	66.7

MOST INTERCEPTIONS, GAME

PLAYER	TEAM	GAME	INT
1 Rod Martin	OAK	XV	3
2 Randy Beverly	NYJ	III	2
= Chuck Howley	DAL	V	2
= Jake Scott	MIA	VII	2
= Barry Wilburn	WAS	XXII	2
= Brad Edwards	WAS	XXVI	2
= Thomas Everett	DAL	XXVII	2
= Larry Brown	DAL	XXX	2
= Darrien Gordon*	DEN	XXXIII	2

DID YOU KNOW?
Jim Plunkett and Joe Montana are the only quarterbacks in Super Bowl history to attempt at least 40 passes without throwing an interception.

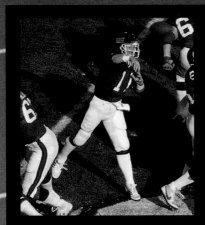

IN THE GROOVE

The Giants trailed 3-0 as Phil Simms took the field for the first time in Super Bowl XXI. Simms completed all 6 of his passes on the ensuing 78-yard drive to stake the Giants to a 7-3 lead. Simms's early success proved not to be a fluke. He completed 22 of his 25 pass attempts for a Super Bowl-record 88 percent completion percentage en route to the Giants' 39-20 victory over the Denver Broncos. Simms passed for 268 yards and 3 touchdowns, with no interceptions, in what would turn out to be his lone Super Bowl appearance (he was injured for the Giants' Super Bowl XXV victory).

TIME OUT

MOST RECEIVING TOUCHDOWNS, GAME

	PLAYER	TEAM	GAME	TDS
1	Jerry Rice*	SF	XXIV	3
=	Jerry Rice*	SF	XXIX	3
3	Max McGee	GB	I	2
=	Bill Miller	OAK	II	2
=	John Stallworth	PIT	XIII	2
=	Cliff Branch	OAK	XV	2
=	Dan Ross	CIN	XVI	2
=	Roger Craig	SF	XIX	2
=	Ricky Sanders	WAS	XXII	2
=	Michael Irvin	DAL	XXVII	2
=	Ricky Watters*	SF	XXIX	2
=	Antonio Freeman*	GB	XXXII	2

Ricky Sanders's touchdowns covered 80 and 50 yards. Both came in the second quarter.

LONGEST FIELD GOALS

	PLAYER	TEAM	GAME	YDS
1	Steve Christie*	BUF	XXVIII	54
2	Jason Elam*	DEN	XXXII	51
3	Jeff Wilkins*	RAM	XXXVI	50
4	Jan Stenerud	KC	IV	48
=	Rich Karlis	DEN	XXI	48
=	Adam Vinatieri*	NE	XXXVI	48
7	Jim Turner	DEN	XII	47
=	Matt Stover*	BAL	XXXV	47
9	Chris Bahr	OAK	XV	46
=	Norm Johnson	PIT	XXX	46

Super Bowl XXXVI featured 2 of the 6 longest field goals in Super Bowl history, including Adam Vinatieri's game-winning 48-yard field goal as time expired.

DIALING LONG DISTANCE

Buffalo's Steve Christie made all 3 of his Super Bowl field-goal attempts, including a record 54-yard kick in Super Bowl XXVIII against the Cowboys.

*Active through 2001 season

SUPER BOWL

MOST VICTORIES

TEAM	VICTORIES
1 San Francisco 49ers	5
= Dallas Cowboys	5
3 Pittsburgh Steelers	4
4 Green Bay Packers	3
= Oakland Raiders	3
= Washington Redskins	3
7 New York Giants	2
= Miami Dolphins	2
= Denver Broncos	2
10 Baltimore Ravens	1
= Chicago Bears	1
= New York Jets	1
= Baltimore Colts	1
= Kansas City Chiefs	1
= St. Louis Rams	1
= New England Patriots	1

LARGEST MARGIN OF VICTORY

SUPER BOWL	SCORE	MARGIN
1 XXIV	SF 55, DEN 10	45
2 XX	CHI 46, NE 10	36
3 XXVII	DAL 52, BUF 17	35
4 XXII	WAS 42, DEN 10	32
5 XVIII	RAI 38, WAS 9	29
6 XXXV	BAL 34, NYG 7	27
7 I	GB 35, KC 10	25
8 XXIX	SF 49, SD 26	23
9 XIX	SF 38, MIA 16	22
10 VI	DAL 24, MIA 3	21

CLOSEST MARGIN OF VICTORY

SUPER BOWL	SCORE	MARGIN
1 XXV	NYG 20, BUF 19	1
2 V	BAC 16, DAL 13	3
= XXXVI	NE 20, RAM 17	3
4 X	PIT 21, DAL 17	4
= XIII	PIT 35, DAL 31	4
= XXIII	SF 20, CIN 16	4
7 XVI	SF 26, CIN 21	5
8 VII	MIA 14, WAS 7	7
= XXXII	DEN 31, GB 24	7
= XXXIV	RAM 23, TEN 16	7

JOHNNY ON THE SPOT
John Taylor's 10-yard touchdown catch with 34 seconds remaining capped a 92-yard drive and gave the 49ers a 20-16 victory over the Bengals in Super Bowl XXIII.

DID YOU KNOW?
Four of the six Super Bowl games played one week after the conference title games have been decided by 10 points or less (66.7 percent), compared to only 7 of the 30 games (23.3 percent) played after a two-week break.

STAUBACH IN CHARGE
Roger Staubach guided the Dallas Cowboys to NFL championships in Super Bowls VI and XII.

MOST APPEARANCES

TEAM	GAMES
1 Dallas Cowboys	8
2 Denver Broncos	6
3 San Francisco 49ers	5
= Pittsburgh Steelers	5
= Washington Redskins	5
= Miami Dolphins	5
7 Green Bay Packers	4
= Oakland Raiders	4
= Buffalo Bills	4
= Minnesota Vikings	4

Active through 2001 season

THE PERFECT TACKLE

A Super Bowl game has never gone into overtime. But it probably would have happened in Super Bowl XXXIV were it not for a textbook tackle by Rams linebacker Mike Jones. St. Louis had a 23-16 lead, but the Titans had reached the Rams' 10-yard line with six seconds left. With no time outs, Titans quarterback Steve McNair attempted a quick pass to Kevin Dyson, who caught the ball in stride at the Rams' 3. However, Jones reacted quickly and stepped up to tackle Dyson at the 1-yard line as time expired.

TIME OUT

MOST POINTS

TEAM	SUPER BOWL	POINTS
1 SF	XXIV	55
2 DAL	XXVII	52
3 SF	XXIX	49
4 CHI	XX	46
5 WAS	XXII	42
6 NYG	XXI	39
7 RAI	XVIII	38
= SF	XIX	38
9 WAS	XXVI	37
10 GB	I	35
= PIT	XIII	35
= GB	XXXI	35

MOST POINTS, BOTH TEAMS

SUPER BOWL	SCORE	PTS
1 XXIX	SF 49, SD 26	75
2 XXVII	DAL 52, BUF 17	69
3 XIII	PIT 35, DAL 31	66
4 XXIV	SF 55, DEN 10	65
5 XXVI	WAS 37, BUF 24	61
6 XXI	NYG 39, DEN 20	59
7 XX	CHI 46, NE 10	56
= XXXI	GB 35, NE 21	56
9 XXXII	DEN 31, GB 24	55
10 XIX	SF 38, MIA 16	54

MOST POINTS, HALF

SUPER BOWL	TEAMS	HALF	PTS
1 XXII	WAS	1	35
2 XXI	NYG	2	30
3 XIX	SF	1	28
= XXIV	SF	2	28
= XXVII	DAL	1	28
= XXIX	SF	1	28
7 XXIX	SF	2	27
= XXXI	GB	1	27
9 XXVI	BUF	2	24
= XXVII	DAL	2	24
= XXVIII	DAL	2	24
= XXXV	BAL	2	24

WHAT A HALF!
Phil McConkey's 6-yard touchdown catch, off Mark Bavaro's deflection, is a memorable part of the Giants' 30-point second half en route to their 39-20 Super Bowl XXI victory.

TRIVIA TIME
The Washington Redskins won three Super Bowls during a 10-year period (1982–1991) with three different starting quarterbacks. Can you name them?

A: Joe Theismann, Doug Williams, and Mark Rypien.

KINGDOM OF TROY

Troy Aikman, who posted a 3-0 record in Super Bowls, completed 70 percent of his passes, a Super Bowl record.

MOST POINTS, QUARTER, BOTH TEAMS

	SUPER BOWL	TEAMS	QTR	PTS
1	XXII	WAS-DEN	2	35
2	XXXIII	DEN-ATL	4	30
3	XIII	PIT-DAL	4	28
4	XIX	SF-MIA	2	27
5	XXVI	WAS-BUF	3	24
=	XXXI	GB-NE	1	24
7	XXI	NYG-DEN	4	23
8	XXIX	SF-SD	3	22
9	X	PIT-DAL	4	21
=	XIII	PIT-DAL	2	21
=	XX	CHI-NE	3	21
=	XXIV	SF-DEN	3	21
=	XXVII	DAL-BUF	1	21
=	XXVII	DAL-BUF	4	21
=	XXIX	SF-SD	1	21
=	XXXV	BAL-NYG	3	21

Most of these high-scoring quarters occurred during blowouts. The Redskins, for example, scored all 35 points in the second quarter of their Super Bowl XXII rout of the Broncos, and Denver coasted to an easy victory over the Falcons in Super Bowl XXXIII. The high-scoring quarter in Super Bowl XIII, however, produced an exciting finish. The Steelers scored 2 touchdowns 19 seconds apart in the middle of the fourth quarter to take a 35-17 lead. The Cowboys scored on their next two possessions to cut the lead to 35-31 with 22 seconds left, but Pittsburgh recovered the ensuing onside kick to clinch the game.

MOST POINTS, HALF, BOTH TEAMS

	SUPER BOWL	TEAMS	HALF	PTS
1	XXII	WAS-DEN	1	45
2	XIX	SF-MIA	1	44
=	XXVI	WAS-BUF	2	44
4	XXXI	GB-NE	1	41
5	XXI	NYG-DEN	2	40
6	XXVII	DAL-BUF	1	38
=	XXIX	SF-SD	1	38
8	XXIX	SF-SD	2	37
9	XXIV	SF-DEN	2	35
10	XIII	PIT-DAL	2	31
=	XXVII	DAL-BUF	2	31
=	XXXII	DEN-GB	1	31
=	XXXV	BAL-NYG	2	31

MOST POINTS, QUARTER

	SUPER BOWL	TEAMS	QTR	PTS
1	XXII	WAS	2	35
2	XIX	SF	2	21
=	XX	CHI	3	21
=	XXVII	DAL	4	21
5	XXI	NYG	3	17
=	XXVI	WAS	2	17
=	XXXI	GB	2	17
=	XXXIII	DEN	4	17
9	XI	OAK	2	16
10	Twenty-eight teams			14

QUALITY TIME

The Redskins had the ball for just 5 minutes and 47 seconds during the second quarter of Super Bowl XXII, but that proved to be more than enough time for Doug Williams. Washington ran 18 plays, 5 of which resulted in touchdowns, to turn a 10-0 deficit into a 35-10 lead. The Redskins went on to a 42-10 victory over Denver, and Williams, the first African-American to start a Super Bowl at quarterback, earned MVP honors after completing 18 of 29 passes for 340 yards and 4 touchdowns.

TIME OUT

HIGHEST PASSER RATING, CAREER

	PLAYER	RATING
1	Bart Starr	104.8
2	Joe Montana	95.6
3	Ken Anderson	93.5
4	Kurt Warner*	92.3
5	Joe Theismann	91.4
6	Troy Aikman	88.3
7	Brett Favre*	87.7
8	Steve Young	85.8
9	Warren Moon	84.9
10	Ken Stabler	84.2

MOST PASSING YARDS, GAME

	PLAYER	TEAM VS OPP	DATE	YARDS
1	Bernie Kosar	CLE vs. NYJ	1/3/87	489
2	Dan Fouts	SD vs. MIA	1/2/82	433
3	Jeff George*	MIN vs. RAM	1/16/00	423
4	Dan Marino	MIA at BUF	12/30/95	422
5	Dan Marino	MIA vs. PIT	1/6/85	421
6	Kurt Warner*	RAM vs. TEN	1/30/00	414
7	Jim Kelly	BUF at CLE	1/6/90	405
8	Don Strock	MIA vs. SD	1/2/82	403
9	Daryle Lamonica	OAK at NYJ	12/29/68	401
10	Kurt Warner*	RAM vs. MIN	1/16/00	391

RECEPTIONS, CAREER

	PLAYER	RECEPTIONS
1	Jerry Rice*	137
2	Michael Irvin	87
3	Andre Reed	85
4	Thurman Thomas	76
5	Cliff Branch	73
6	Fred Biletnikoff	70
7	Art Monk	69
8	Drew Pearson	67
9	Tony Nathan	65
10	Cris Carter*	63
=	Roger Craig	63

Jerry Rice's totals include a huge game (9 receptions for 183 yards) during the 2001 playoffs in which the 39-year-old Rice became the oldest player ever to score a touchdown in the postseason.

SUPER BOWL STARR
Quarterback Bart Starr, who guided the Green Bay Packers to five NFL championships, was named the most valuable player of Super Bowls I and II.

DID YOU KNOW?
Don Strock, who passed for 403 yards in the Dolphins' 41-38 overtime loss to the Chargers in a 1981 AFC Divisional Playoff Game, did not start. He replaced David Woodley in the second quarter.

MOST RECEPTIONS, GAME

PLAYER	TEAM VS OPP	DATE	YARDS
1 Kellen Winslow	SD at MIA	1/2/82	13
= Thurman Thomas	BUF at CLE	1/6/90	13
= Shannon Sharpe*	DEN at RAI	1/9/94	13
= Chad Morton*	NO at MIN	1/6/01	13
5 Raymond Berry	BAC at NYG	12/28/58	12
= Michael Irvin	DAL at SF	1/15/95	12
7 Dante Lavelli	CLE vs. RAM	12/24/50	11
= Dan Ross	CIN vs. SF	1/24/82	11
= Franco Harris	PIT vs. SD	1/9/83	11
= Steve Watson	DEN vs. PIT	12/30/84	11
= John L. Williams	SEA at CIN	12/31/88	11
= Jerry Rice*	SF vs. CIN	1/22/89	11
= Ernest Givins	HOU vs. PIT	12/31/89	11
= Amp Lee	MIN vs. CHI	1/1/95	11
= Jay Novacek	DAL vs. GB	1/8/95	11
= O.J. McDuffie	MIA at BUF	12/30/95	11
= Jerry Rice*	SF vs. GB	1/6/96	11

Of the four players who caught 13 passes in a playoff game, Kellen Winslow is the only one whose team prevailed.

JUST IN TIME
Thanks to 489 passing yards by quarterback Bernie Kosar, the Browns overcame a 10-point deficit with less than five minutes remaining and went on to defeat the New York Jets 23-20 in overtime.

GREAT EFFORT

TIME OUT

On a humid night in January, 1982, third-year tight end Kellen Winslow delivered one of the greatest performances in football history. Winslow (number 80, left) caught 13 passes for 166 yards and 1 touchdown, and despite heat exhaustion, he came off the bench to block a potential game-winning field goal on the final play of regulation. San Diego went on to defeat Miami 41-38 in overtime in a game that ranks as one of the NFL's greatest. Though a knee injury shortened his career (1979–1987), Winslow is arguably the greatest tight end in the history of the NFL and a member of the Pro Football Hall of Fame.

*Active through 2001 season

MOST RUSHING YARDS, GAME

	PLAYER	TEAM VS OPP	DATE	YARDS
1	Eric Dickerson	RAM vs. DAL	1/4/86	248
2	Lamar Smith*	MIA vs. IND	12/30/00	209
3	Keith Lincoln	SD vs. BOS	1/5/64	206
4	Timmy Smith	WAS vs. DEN	1/31/88	204
5	Lawrence McCutcheon	RAM vs. STC	12/27/75	202
=	Freeman McNeil	NYJ at CIN	1/9/83	202
7	Terrell Davis*	DEN vs. MIA	1/9/99	199
8	Steve Van Buren	PHI at RAM	12/18/49	196
9	Marcus Allen	RAI vs. WAS	1/22/84	191
10	Terrell Davis*	DEN vs. JAX	12/27/97	184

As is usually the case with a good running game, all of these players' teams were victorious in their postseason games.

MOST RUSHING YARDS, CAREER

	PLAYER	YARDS
1	Emmitt Smith*	1,586
2	Franco Harris	1,556
3	Thurman Thomas	1,442
4	Tony Dorsett	1,383
5	Marcus Allen	1,347
6	Terrell Davis*	1,140
7	John Riggins	996
8	Larry Csonka	891
9	Chuck Foreman	860
10	Roger Craig	841

Terrell Davis owns the NFL postseason records for highest rushing average (5.6 yards per carry) and yards per game (142.5).

NFL NOTEBOOK

Emmitt Smith and Terrell Davis each have accrued seven 100-yard rushing games in postseason play. Smith has played in 17 games, while Davis has rushed for at least 100 yards in 7 of his 8 postseason games.

BIG, BAD BRUCE

Despite being the focus of his opponents' pass-blocking schemes, Bruce Smith has racked up an NFL-record 14½ sacks in 19 career postseason games.

TRIVIA TIME
Thurman Thomas and Emmitt Smith share the NFL postseason record for career touchdowns with 21. Do you know who is next in line with 20?

A: Jerry Rice

MOST INTERCEPTIONS, CAREER

PLAYER	INTERCEPTIONS
1 Ronnie Lott	9
= Bill Simpson	9
= Charlie Waters	9
4 Lester Hayes	8
5 Willie Brown	7
= Dennis Thurman	7
7 Bobby Bryant	6
= Eric Davis*	6
= Glen Edwards	6
= Darrell Green*	6
= Cliff Harris	6
= Vernon Perry	6
= Aeneas Williams*	6

NOT JUST A HARD TACKLER
Ronnie Lott is remembered for his hard-hitting style throughout an illustrious 14-year career that landed him in the Pro Football Hall of Fame, but his 9 interceptions in postseason play have not been surpassed.

MOST SACKS, CAREER#

PLAYER	SACKS
1 Bruce Smith*	14.5
2 Reggie White	12.0
3 Charles Haley	11.0
4 Richard Dent	10.5
5 Trace Armstrong*	10.0
= Charles Mann	10.0
= Tony Tolbert	10.0
8 Neil Smith	9.5
9 Jeff Wright	9.0
10 Kevin Greene	8.5

#Sacks became an official statistic in 1982.

TIME OUT — AFL GREAT

Running back Keith Lincoln was just a rookie in 1961, when the Chargers reached the AFL Championship Game but lost to the Oilers. Two years later, Lincoln took matters into his own hands. Against the Patriots in the 1963 AFL Championship Game, Lincoln rushed for 206 yards on 13 carries, had 7 receptions for 123 yards, and completed his lone pass attempt for 20 yards. Lincoln's 67-yard touchdown run in the first quarter staked the Chargers to a 14-0 lead, and he added a 25-yard touchdown catch in the fourth quarter to lead the Chargers to a 51-10 victory and their only championship.

Active through 2001 season

TOP 10 ODDS & ENDS

TOP OF THE MOUNTAIN
Don Shula is carried off the field after the Dolphins'
19-14 victory at Philadelphia on November 14,
1993—the 325th victory of his career, an NFL record.
Shula also coached the only perfect team in NFL
history (his 1972 Dolphins went 17-0).

BEFORE HE WAS FAMOUS...
...John Madden was a coach, and a good one. He posted the second-best winning percentage in NFL history during his 10 seasons in Oakland.

MOST VICTORIES, HEAD COACH

	COACH	TEAM(S)	WINS
1	Don Shula	BAC/MIA	347
2	George Halas	CHI	324
3	Tom Landry	DAL	270
4	Curly Lambeau	GB/CHC/WAS	229
5	Chuck Noll	PIT	209
6	Chuck Knox	RAM/BUF/SEA	193
7	Dan Reeves*	DEN/NYG/ATL	188
8	Paul Brown	CLE/CIN	170
9	Bud Grant	MIN	168
10	Marty Schottenheimer*	CLE/KC/WAS	158

Unlike player statistics, coaches' records include postseason games. Don Shula's total, for example, includes 19 postseason victories.

HIGHEST WINNING PERCENTAGE, HEAD COACH#

	COACH	TEAM(S)	W-L-T	PCT
1	Vince Lombardi	GB/WAS	105-35-6	.740
2	John Madden	OAK	112-39-7	.731
3	Joe Gibbs	WAS	140-65-0	.683
4	George Allen	RAM/WAS	118-54-5	.681
5	George Halas	CHI	324-151-31	.671
6	Don Shula	BAC/MIA	347-173-6	.665
7	George Seifert*	SF/CAR	124-67-0	.649
8	Curly Lambeau	GB/CHC/WAS	229-134-22	.623
9	Bill Walsh	SF	102-63-1	.617
10	Mike Holmgren*	GB/SEA	108-67-0	.617

#Minimum 100 victories

TRIVIA TIME
Paul Brown is one of only two coaches in NFL history to lead his club to the postseason in each of his first six seasons as a head coach. Can you name the other?

A: Bill Cowher

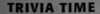

ACTIVE VICTORIES, HEAD COACH

COACH	WINS
1 Dan Reeves*	188
2 Marty Schottenheimer*	158
3 Jim Mora*	125
4 George Seifert*	124
5 Mike Holmgren*	108
6 Bill Cowher*	105
7 Dick Vermeil*	88
8 Mike Shanahan*	87
9 Jeff Fisher*	68
10 Tom Coughlin*	66

MOST SEASONS, HEAD COACH

COACH	TEAM(S)	SEASONS
1 George Halas	CHI	40
2 Curly Lambeau	GB/CHC/WAS	33
= Don Shula	BAC/MIA	33
4 Tom Landry	DAL	29
5 Chuck Noll	PIT	23
= Steve Owen	NYG	23
7 Chuck Knox	RAM/BUF/SEA	22
8 Paul Brown	CLE/CIN	21
= Dan Reeves*	DEN/NYG/ATL	21
10 Weeb Ewbank	BAC/NYJ	20

A STOIC WINNER

The Dallas Cowboys posted an NFL-record 20 consecutive winning seasons (1966–1985) and won 13 divisional titles and 5 NFC championships under the tutelage of Tom Landry.

MOST POSTSEASON VICTORIES, HEAD COACH

COACH	TEAM(S)	WINS
1 Tom Landry	DAL	20
2 Don Shula	BAC/MIA	19
3 Joe Gibbs	WAS	16
= Chuck Noll	PIT	16
5 Marv Levy	BUF	11
= Bill Parcells	NYG/NE/NYJ	11
7 Bud Grant	MIN	10
= Dan Reeves*	DEN/NYG/ATL	10
= George Seifert*	SF	10
= Bill Walsh	SF	10

AN IMMEDIATE WINNER

Vince Lombardi's career as a head coach lasted only 10 seasons, but he left a lasting impression that extends beyond the NFL. Lombardi was a Giants assistant coach when he was hired to coach the Green Bay Packers in 1959. He took over a team that had won just one game in 1958, but Lombardi had them playing for the 1960 NFL championship. The Packers would go on to win the NFL title five times in the next seven seasons before Lombardi took a year off. He coached the Redskins in 1969 before his death in 1970.

TIME OUT

* Active through 2001 season

TIME OUT

STILL STANDING

The Chicago Cubs' Wrigley Field is not the only historic sports venue in the Windy City. Soldier Field, named in honor of America's World War I veterans, hosted its first game in 1924 as the University of Notre Dame defeated Northwestern University. The first professional game, between the Bears and then-crosstown rival Cardinals, took place on November 11, 1926. The Bears still played their home games at Wrigley Field through 1970, when they officially made Soldier Field their home.

STADIUMS THAT HAVE HOSTED PRO BOWLS

	STADIUM	CITY	GMS
1	Aloha Stadium	Honolulu	23
=	Memorial Coliseum	Los Angeles	23
3	Gilmore Stadium	Los Angeles	2
4	Arrowhead Stadium	Kansas City	1
=	Kingdome	Seattle	1
=	Superdome	New Orleans	1
=	Orange Bowl	Miami	1
=	Polo Grounds	New York	1
=	Shibe Park	Philadelphia	1
=	Tampa Stadium	Tampa Bay	1
=	Texas Stadium	Dallas	1
=	Wrigley Field	Los Angeles	1

WHO SAYS L.A. DOESN'T LIKE FOOTBALL?
The Rose Bowl owns the distinction of hosting the five largest crowds in Super Bowl history.

TRIVIA TIME
The largest regular-season crowd in NFL history was 102,368. Can you name the stadium that hosted that gathering?

A: The Los Angeles Memorial Coliseum on November 10, 1957, for a game between the Rams and 49ers.

STADIUMS THAT HAVE HOSTED SUPER BOWLS

	STADIUM	CITY	GAMES
1	Superdome	New Orleans	6
2	Orange Bowl	Miami	5
=	Rose Bowl	Pasadena	5
4	Pro Player Stadium	Miami	3
=	Tulane Stadium	New Orleans	3
6	Georgia Dome	Atlanta	2
=	Memorial Coliseum	Los Angeles	2
=	Qualcomm Stadium	San Diego	2
=	Tampa Stadium	Tampa Bay	2
10	Six stadiums with		1

The city of New Orleans has hosted the most Super Bowls (nine, with six at the Louisiana Superdome and three at Tulane Stadium), followed by Miami (eight), and Los Angeles (seven, including five at the Rose Bowl). No other city has hosted the game more than twice.

OLDEST STADIUMS

	STADIUM	CITY	YEAR OPENED
1	Soldier Field	Chicago	1924
2	Lambeau Field	Green Bay	1957
3	3Com Park	San Francisco	1958
=	Sun Devil Stadium	Tempe	1958
5	Network Associates Coliseum	Oakland	1966
6	Qualcomm Stadium	San Diego	1967
7	Texas Stadium	Dallas	1971
=	Veterans Stadium	Philadelphia	1971
9	Arrowhead Stadium	Kansas City	1972
10	Ralph Wilson Stadium	Buffalo	1973

The Los Angeles Memorial Coliseum, formerly the home of the Rams (1946–1979) and the Raiders (1982–1994), opened in 1923.

NFL NOTEBOOK

The first Pro Bowl matched the NFL-champion New York Giants against a team of pro all-stars at Los Angeles's Wrigley Field in 1939. No, that's not a misprint—the Wrigley family spent their winters in California, where they owned another stadium bearing their name.

LONGEST POSTSEASON OVERTIME GAMES

	SCORE	DATE	LENGTH
1	MIA 27, KC 24	12/25/71	82:40
2	DAT 20, HOU 17	12/23/62	77:54
3	CLE 23, NYJ 20	1/3/87	77:02
4	OAK 37, BAC 31	12/24/77	75:43
5	SD 41, MIA 38	1/2/82	73:52
6	GB 13, BAC 10	12/26/65	73:39
7	ATL 30, MIN 27	1/17/99	71:52
8	MIA 23, IND 17	12/30/00	71:16
9	KC 27, PIT 24	1/8/94	71:03
10	BAC 23, NYG 17	12/28/58	68:15

During the regular season, if the teams remain tied after the 15-minute overtime period, the game ends in a tie. During the postseason, the teams keep playing until one scores, as happened in the four double-overtime games that top this list.

CAN'T GET ANY LONGER

Mike Quick's 99-yard touchdown catch in 1985 is the longest play from scrimmage in NFL overtime history.

MERRY CHRISTMAS, DOLPHINS FANS

He's remembered for his botched pass attempt in Super Bowl VII, but a season earlier Garo Yepremian's 37-yard field goal in the second overtime on Christmas Day ended the longest game in NFL history.

DID YOU KNOW?
The St. Louis/Phoenix Cardinals hold the NFL record by playing 110 consecutive games without an overtime (December 7, 1986–December 19, 1993).

MOST OVERTIME GAMES IN A SEASON

TEAM		SEASON	GAMES
1	Green Bay Packers	1983	5
2	Denver Broncos	1985	4
=	Cleveland Browns	1989	4
=	Minnesota Vikings	1994	4
=	Arizona Cardinals	1995	4
=	Minnesota Vikings	1995	4
=	Arizona Cardinals	1997	4
=	San Francisco 49ers	2001	4
9	Many teams with		3

The Packers won just two of their five overtime games in 1983, including a 23-20 loss to the Detroit Lions, and finished just one game behind the Lions for the NFC Central title.

MOST COMMON FINISH, OVERTIME GAME

DECIDED BY		TIMES
1	Field Goal	219
2	Touchdown Pass	37
3	Touchdown Run	22
4	Tied Game	15
5	Interception Return	13
6	Fake Field Goal/TD Pass	2
=	Fumble Return	2
8	Kickoff Return	1
=	Punt Return	1
=	Fake Field Goal/TD Run	1
=	Blocked Field Goal Return	1
=	Blocked FG/Recover by Kicker	1
=	Blocked FG/Recover by Kicking Team	1
=	Safety	1

On September 7, 1980, Packers kicker Chester Marcol's 35-yard field-goal try was blocked by the Bears' Alan Page. The ball bounced right back to Marcol, who lumbered 24 yards for the game-winning touchdown.

LONGEST TOUCHDOWNS TO END OVERTIME GAME

	PLAYER(S)	TEAM VS OPP	DATE	PLAY	YDS
1	Ron Jaworski to Mike Quick	PHI vs. ATL	11/10/85	Pass	99
2	Garrison Hearst*	SF vs. NYJ	9/6/98	Run	96
3	Dave Williams	CHI at DET	11/27/80	Kick Return	95
4	Tamarick Vanover	KC vs. SD	10/9/95	Punt Return	86
5	Troy Aikman to Raghib Ismail*	DAL at WAS	9/12/99	Pass	76
6	Lorenzo Lynch	ARI vs. SEA	10/29/95	Interception	72
7	Danny Kanell* to Chris Calloway	NYG at DET	10/19/97	Pass	68
8	Warren Moon to Cris Carter*	MIN vs. CHI	12/1/94	Pass	65
9	Louis Wright	DEN vs. SD	11/17/85	Blocked FG	60
=	Herschel Walker	DAL at NE	11/15/87	Run	60

QUICKEST SCORES TO END OVERTIME GAMES#

	PLAYER(S)	TEAM VS OPP	DATE	PLAY	TIME
1	Mike Brown*	CHI vs. SF	10/28/01	Interception	0:16
2	Doug Brien*	NO vs. SEA	11/16/97	Field Goal	0:17
3	Dave Williams	CHI at DET	11/27/80	Kick Return	0:21
4	Johnie Cooks	BAC at NE	9/4/83	Fumble Ret.	0:30
5	Elvis Patterson	NYG at PHI	9/29/85	Interception	0:55
6	Jim Breech	CIN vs. BUF	9/14/86	Field Goal	0:56
7	Jim Breech	CIN vs. RAI	9/13/92	Field Goal	1:01
8	Terry Bradshaw to John Stallworth	PIT vs. CIN	9/19/82	Pass	1:08
9	Paul McFadden	NYG at DET	10/30/88	Field Goal	1:13
10	Norm Johnson	SEA vs. KC	11/27/83	Field Goal	1:36
=	Gus Frerotte* to Michael Westbrook*	WAS vs. ARI	9/14/97	Pass	1:36

#Touchdowns except where noted

WORKING OVERTIME

Pinned at their 4-yard line, the 49ers handed the ball to Garrison Hearst, hoping for a few yards. Instead, Hearst ended the game by taking the handoff and outrunning the Jets down the right sideline for a 96-yard touchdown—the longest run ever in overtime—that gave San Francisco a 36-30 victory in the 1998 season opener. Hearst surprised the 49ers again in 2001 by returning from a career-threatening injury and running for 1,206 yards, a performance that earned him comeback player of the year honors for the second time in his career.

TIME OUT

* Active through 2001 season

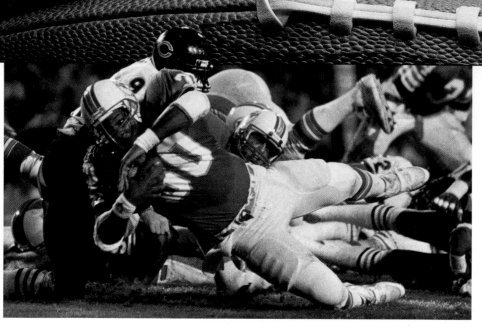

MOST WINS ON NFL MONDAY NIGHT FOOTBALL

	TEAM	WINS
1	Miami	36
2	San Francisco	35
=	Dallas	35
4	Oakland	34
5	Pittsburgh	29
6	Washington	24
7	Minnesota	21
=	Denver	21
9	St. Louis	20
10	Green Bay	18

BEST WINNING PERCENTAGE ON NFL MONDAY NIGHT FOOTBALL#

	TEAM	W-L-T	PCT
1	Seattle	12-6	.667
2	Oakland	34-19-1	.639
3	San Francisco	35-20	.637
4	Pittsburgh	29-18	.617
5	Dallas	35-26	.574
6	Indianapolis	12-9	.571
7	Kansas City	17-13	.567
8	Miami	36-29	.554
9	Cleveland	13-11	.542
10	San Diego	14-12	.538

#Minimum 10 games

NFL NOTEBOOK
In the 32-year history (1970–2001) of *NFL Monday Night Football*, no team has appeared every season. The Dolphins and Raiders share the distinction for appearing on Monday night in all but one season.

MOST WATCHED GAMES

	PROGRAM	TEAMS	DATE	NETWORK	VIEWERS
1	Super Bowl XXX	DAL-PIT	1/28/96	NBC	138,488,000
2	Super Bowl XXVIII	DAL-BUF	1/30/94	NBC	134,800,000
3	Super Bowl XXXII	DEN-GB	1/25/98	NBC	133,400,000
=	Super Bowl XXVII	DAL-BUF	1/31/93	NBC	133,400,000
5	Super Bowl XXXVI	NE-RAM	2/3/02	FOX	131,700,000
6	Super Bowl XXXV	BAL-NYG	1/28/01	CBS	131,200,000
7	Super Bowl XXXIV	RAM-TEN	1/30/00	ABC	130,744,800
8	Super Bowl XXXI	GB-NE	1/26/97	FOX	128,900,000
9	Super Bowl XXXIII	DEN-ATL	1/31/99	FOX	127,500,000
10	Super Bowl XX	CHI-NE	1/26/86	NBC	127,000,000

HIGHEST RATED GAMES

	PROGRAM	TEAMS	DATE	NETWORK	SHARE	RATING
1	Super Bowl XVI	SF-CIN	1/24/82	CBS	73%	49.1
2	Super Bowl XVII	MIA-WAS	1/30/83	NBC	69%	48.6
3	Super Bowl XX	CHI-NE	1/26/86	NBC	70%	48.3
4	Super Bowl XII	DAL-DEN	1/15/78	CBS	67%	47.2
5	Super Bowl XIII	PIT-DAL	1/21/79	NBC	74%	47.1
6	Super Bowl XVIII	RAI-WAS	1/22/84	CBS	71%	46.4
7	Super Bowl XIX	SF-MIA	1/20/85	ABC	63%	46.4
8	Super Bowl XIV	PIT-RAM	1/20/80	CBS	67%	46.3
9	Super Bowl XXX	DAL-PIT	1/28/96	NBC	68%	46.0
10	Super Bowl XXI	NYG-DEN	1/25/87	CBS	66%	45.8

A share reflects the percentage of televisions turned on that tuned into the game. Rating reflects the overall percentage of viewers.

TRIVIA TIME
Who holds the record for most rushing yards in a game on *NFL Monday Night Football?*

A: On November 30, 1987, Bo Jackson of the Los Angeles Raiders ran for 221 yards as the Raiders defeated the Seattle Seahawks.

1970S RAIDERS ON MONDAY=WINS

During the height of the Oakland Raiders' dominance during the 1970s and early 1980s, they were unbeatable on *NFL Monday Night Football*. How good were the Raiders in their heyday? From 1975 until losing to the San Diego Chargers in the last week of the 1981 season, the Raiders won 14 consecutive Monday night games. Ken Stabler was the quarterback for the Raiders' first nine victories of the streak, four of which were road games. In fact, upon conclusion of the 1981 season, the Raiders owned an impressive 18-2-1 record on Mondays. Since 1981, however, the Raiders are 16-17 on *NFL Monday Night Football*, including just a 3-8 record since 1995.

TIME OUT

DEFENSIVE STAND
The 49ers used a staunch defensive effort to stop the Bengals on three successive plays from the 1-yard line before a record Super Bowl audience.

PLAYERS

SUPER BOWL XXXV MVP
Ray Lewis earned NFL defensive player of the year honors in 2000 en route to the Ravens' Super Bowl XXXV title.

MOST RECENT ASSOCIATED PRESS MVP

SEASON	PLAYER	TEAM
2001	Kurt Warner*	RAM
2000	Marshall Faulk*	RAM
1999	Kurt Warner*	RAM
1998	Terrell Davis*	DEN
1997	Brett Favre*	GB
=	Barry Sanders	DET
1996	Brett Favre*	GB
1995	Brett Favre*	GB
1994	Steve Young	SF
1993	Emmitt Smith*	DAL
1992	Steve Young	SF

The *Associated Press* award, which has been presented since 1957, is the most prestigious of the honors given by media organizations.

MOST RECENT OFFENSIVE PLAYER OF THE YEAR

SEASON	PLAYER	TEAM
2001	Marshall Faulk*	RAM
2000	Marshall Faulk*	RAM
1999	Marshall Faulk*	RAM
1998	Terrell Davis*	DEN
1997	Barry Sanders	DET
1996	Terrell Davis*	DEN
1995	Brett Favre*	GB
1994	Barry Sanders	DET
1993	Jerry Rice*	SF
1992	Steve Young*	SF

Only Earl Campbell (1978–1980) has matched Faulk's three consecutive offensive player of the year awards.

MOST RECENT DEFENSIVE PLAYER OF THE YEAR

SEASON	PLAYER	TEAM
2001	Michael Strahan*	NYG
2000	Ray Lewis*	BAL
1999	Warren Sapp*	TB
1998	Reggie White*	GB
1997	Dana Stubblefield*	SF
1996	Bruce Smith*	BUF
1995	Bryce Paup	BUF
1994	Deion Sanders	SF
1993	Rod Woodson*	PIT
1992	Cortez Kennedy	SEA

Giants linebacker Lawrence Taylor is this award's only three-time winner (1981–82, 1987) since its inception in 1966.

DID YOU KNOW?
The *Associated Press* most valuable player award, instituted in 1957, has been awarded to 28 quarterbacks and 14 running backs. The next most honored position? Linebackers (2).

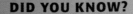

MOST RECENT OFFENSIVE ROOKIE OF THE YEAR

SEASON	PLAYER	TEAM
2001	Anthony Thomas*	CHI
2000	Mike Anderson*	DEN
1999	Edgerrin James*	IND
1998	Randy Moss*	MIN
1997	Warrick Dunn*	TB
1996	Eddie George*	TEN
1995	Curtis Martin*	NE
1994	Marshall Faulk*	IND
1993	Jerome Bettis*	RAM
1992	Carl Pickens	CIN

MOST RECENT DEFENSIVE ROOKIE OF THE YEAR

SEASON	PLAYER	TEAM
2001	Kendrell Bell*	PIT
2000	Brian Urlacher*	CHI
1999	Jevon Kearse*	TEN
1998	Charles Woodson*	OAK
1997	Peter Boulware*	BAL
1996	Simeon Rice*	ARI
1995	Hugh Douglas*	NYJ
1994	Tim Bowens*	MIA
1993	Dana Stubblefield*	SF
1992	Dale Carter*	KC

MOST RECENT COACH OF THE YEAR

SEASON	PLAYER	TEAM
2001	Dick Jauron*	CHI
2000	Jim Haslett*	NO
1999	Dick Vermeil*	RAM
1998	Dan Reeves*	ATL
1997	Jim Fassel*	NYG
1996	Dom Capers	CAR
1995	Ray Rhodes	PHI
1994	Bill Parcells	NE
1993	Dan Reeves*	NYG
1992	Bill Cowher*	PIT

SACK CHAMP

Michael Strahan set an NFL record with 22½ sacks en route to winning the 2001 NFL defensive player of the year award.

* Active through 2001 season

ODDS & ENDS

COLLEGES THAT PRODUCED THE MOST NFL PLAYERS#

	COLLEGE	PLAYERS
1	Notre Dame	429
2	Southern California	359
3	Ohio State	288
4	Penn State	264
5	Michigan	256
6	Nebraska	252
7	Pittsburgh	239
8	UCLA	221
9	Tennessee	213
10	Illinois	210
=	Michigan State	210

#Through 1998

COLLEGES THAT PRODUCED THE MOST NO. 1 PICKS#

	COLLEGE	PLAYERS
1	Notre Dame	5
2	Southern California	4
3	Auburn	3
=	Georgia	3
=	Ohio State	3
=	Stanford	3
=	Texas	3
8	Miami	2
=	Nebraska	2
=	Oklahoma	2
=	Penn State	2
=	Tennessee	2
=	Virginia Tech	2

#1936–2001

Notre Dame's number one picks were Angelo Bertelli (1944), Frank Dancewicz (1946), Leon Hart (1950), Paul Hornung (1956), and Walt Patulski (1972).

COMING INTO HIS OWN

In 2001, Cardinals wide receiver David Boston, selected from Ohio State with the eighth pick of the 1999 draft, had 98 receptions for an NFL-high 1,598 receiving yards and 8 touchdowns.

DID YOU KNOW?

In 1999, the Saints traded six 1999 draft picks and a first- and third-round selection in 2000 to the Redskins so they could move up seven spots in the first round and draft Ricky Williams.

NO. 1 DRAFT PICKS BY POSITION#

	POSITION	PLAYERS
1	Running Back	23
2	Quarterback	19
3	Defensive End	6
4	Defensive Tackle	5
=	Wide Receiver	5
6	Linebacker	3
7	Tackle	2
=	Center	2
9	Guard	1

#1936–2001

BEST PLAYER NICKNAMES

	PLAYER
1	Elroy "Crazylegs" Hirsch
2	Lou "The Toe" Groza
3	Randy "Manster" White
4	"Mean" Joe Greene
5	Dick "Night Train" Lane
6	Ed "Too Tall" Jones
7	Billy "White Shoes" Johnson
8	Ted "Mad Stork" Hendricks
9	William "Refrigerator" Perry
10	Walter "Sweetness" Payton

BEST GROUP NICKNAMES

	NICKNAME	TEAM
1	No-Name Defense	MIA
2	Purple People Eaters	MIN
3	Monsters of the Midway	CHI
4	The Killer B's	MIA
5	Over the Hill Gang	WAS
6	Electric Company	BUF
7	Fun Bunch	WAS
8	Doomsday Defense	DAL
9	Steel Curtain	PIT
10	Kardiac Kids	CLE

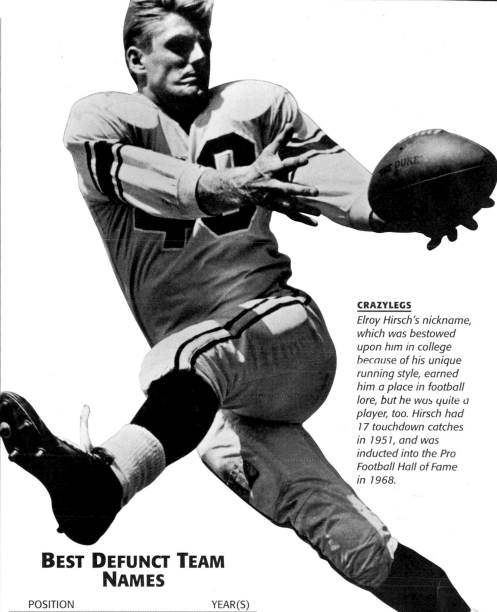

CRAZYLEGS

Elroy Hirsch's nickname, which was bestowed upon him in college because of his unique running style, earned him a place in football lore, but he was quite a player, too. Hirsch had 17 touchdown catches in 1951, and was inducted into the Pro Football Hall of Fame in 1968.

BEST DEFUNCT TEAM NAMES

	POSITION	YEAR(S)
1	Providence Steam Roller	1925–1931
2	Duluth Eskimos	1926–27
3	Tonawanda Kardex	1921
4	Columbus Panhandles	1920–22
5	Evansville Crimson Giants	1921–22
6	Frankford Yellow Jackets	1924–1931
7	Louisville Colonels	1926
8	Dayton Triangles	1920–29
9	Rock Island Independents	1920–25
10	Rochester Jeffersons	1920–25

NFL NOTEBOOK

The NFL franchises that failed were not all losers. In fact, four defunct franchises won NFL titles during the 1920s: Akron Pros (1920); Canton Bulldogs (1922 and 1923); Frankford Yellow Jackets (1926); and Providence Steam Roller (1928).

These are just some of the great football nicknames. What's your favorite?

Numerals in **bold** indicate page with photograph.

Edwards, Glen 37, 77
Elam, Jason 45, **47**, 59, 69
Ellard, Henry 28, 29, 31, 32
Eller, Carl 54
Ellison, Willie 11
Elway, John 16, 17, 18, 22, 24, **26**, 55, 65, 67
Esiason, Boomer 17, 22, 24, 55
Etcheverry, Sam 55
Evans, Fred 54
Everett, Thomas 68
Ewbank, Weeb 81

Farkas, Andy 31
Fair, Terry 51
Farr, Miller 35, 36, 37
Fassel, Jim 89
Faulk, Marshall 13, 14, 15, 40, **42**, 43, 59, 60, 61, 88, 89
Favre, Brett 16, 17, 18, 20, 22, **23**, 24, 31, 55, 58, 64, 67, 68, 74, 88
Feagles, Jeff 49, 57
Fears, Tom **29**, 34
Feathers, Beattie 11, 13
Ferragamo, Vince 17
Fiedler, Jay 23
Filchock, Frank 31
Fisher, Jeff 52, 81
Fleming, Marv 65
Flutie, Doug 23
Foreman, Chuck 43, 64, 76
Fortunato, Joe 54
Foster, Barry 11, 14
Fouts, Dan **16**, 17, 18, 22, 24, 25, 27, 55, 74
Franklin, Bob 37
Franklin, Tony 45
Freeman, Antonio 18, 64, 65, 66, 67, 69
Frerotte, Gus 27, 85
Fryar, Irving 28, 29, 30

Gabriel, Roman 55
Gaines, Clark 29
Gannon, Rich 20, 23, 24, 25, 58
Garcia, Jeff 58
Gardocki, Chris **49**
Gary, Cleveland 13
Gastineau, Mark 38, 39

Gault, Willie 33
Gay, William 39
George, Eddie 14, 15, 59, 66, 89
George, Jeff 26, 74
Gibbs, Joe 80, 81
Gibson, Claude 53
Gilchrist, Cookie 11, 13, 42, 43
Gillom, Horace 48
Givins, Ernest 75
Glasgow, Nesby 53
Glenn, Terry 30
Glick, Frank 34
Gogolak, Pete 46
Gonsoulin, Austin 35
Gordon, Darrien 52, 53, 68
Gossett, Bruce 47
Graham, Kent 27
Graham, Otto **6**, **25**
Gramatica, Martin 45
Grant, Bud 53, 80, 81
Gray, Mel 51
Grbac, Elvis 17, 23, 24
Green, Darrell 36, 56, 57, 58, 77
Green, Roy 51
Green, Trent 19, 27
Greene, Joe 91
Greene, Kevin 39, 54, 77
Griese, Bob 56, 64
Griese, Brian 58
Griffith, Howard 66
Grimes, Billy 53
Groman, Bill 30, **31**, 32
Groza, Lou 46, 47, 91
Gulyanics, George 48
Guy, Ray 49

Haddix, Wayne 37
Hadl, John 18, 27
Haji-Sheikh, Ali 44
Halas, George 80, 81
Haley, Charles 38, 64, 65, 77
Hall, Parker 27
Hansen, Brian 49
Hanson, Jason 59
Hardy, Jim 27
Harmon, Ronnie 67
Harris, Cliff 65, 77
Harris, Dick 37
Harris, Franco 10, 11, 12, 14, 15, 64, 65, 66, 75, 76

Harris, Ronnie 53
Harris, Tim 29
Harrison, Marvin 14, 28, 29, 32
Hart, Jim 27, 31, 56
Hart, Leon 90
Haslett, Jim 89
Hastings, Andre 53, 67
Hasty, James 54
Hayes, Bob 33, 53
Hayes, Lester 34, 35, 77
Haynes, Abner 43
Hearst, Garrison 59, **85**
Heffelfinger, Pudge 6
Hendricks, Ted 91
Hennigan, Charley 28, 29, 31, 32
Hentrich, Craig 48
Herber, Arnie 21
Herron, Mack 53, 60
Hill, Harlon 33
Hirsch, Elroy 30, 32, 35, **91**
Hitchcock, Jimmy 37
Hollis, Mike 46
Holloway, Randy 39
Holmgren, Mike 80, 81
Holt, Torry 29, 32, 64
Hornung, Paul 40, **41**, 43, 90
Houston, Ken 36, **37**
Howard, Darren 38
Howard, Desmond 51, 52, 53, 64
Howley, Chuck 68
Hughes, Tyrone 50, 51
Hultz, Don 54
Humphries, Stan 31, 68
Hunt, Bobby 35
Hutson, Don 30, **31**, **BC**

Irvin, LeRoy 52
Irvin, Michael 29, 32, **33**, 64, 65, 69, 74, 75
Ismail, Raghib 85
Izo, George 31

Jacke, Chris 45
Jackson, Bo 86
Jackson, Harold 32
Jackson, Monte 37
Jackson, Rickey 39, 54, **55**
Jaeger, Jeff 44

James, Edgerrin **14**, 43, 61, 89
James, John 49
James, Lionel 60
Janik, Tom 36
Jauron, Dick 89
Jaworski, Ron 26, 31, 85
Jeffcoat, Jim 39
Jeffers, Patrick 32
Jenkins, MarTay 50, 60
Jenkins, Ronney 50
Jennings, Dave 49
Jeter, Gary 39
Johnson, Billy 52, 53, 91
Johnson, Brad 20, 23, 58
Johnson, Butch 53
Johnson, Charley 26
Johnson, Kenny 37
Johnson, Lee 49
Johnson, Norm 40, 44, 45, 46, 47, 57, 69, 85
Joiner, Charlie 29
Jones, Bert 26
Jones, Deacon **39**
Jones, Dub 43
Jones, Ed 91
Jones, Henry 35, 37
Jones, Homer 33
Jones, Mike **71**
Junkin, Trey 57
Jurgensen, Sonny 16, 17, 18, 31

Kanell, Danny 85
Kapp, Joe 18
Karlis, Rich **45**, 69
Kasay, John 40, 44, 46, 59
Kaufman, Napoleon 13
Kearney, Jim 37
Kearse, Jevon **38**, 89
Kelly, Jim 17, 18, 20, 22, **68**, 74
Kelly, Leroy 12
Kemp, Jack 26, 55
Kennedy, Cortez 88
Kenney, Bill 17
King, Kenny 67
Kinscherf, Carl 48
Kitna, Jon 24, 55
Knight, Curt 47
Knox, Chuck 80, 81
Kosar, Bernie 25, 26, 74, **75**
Kozlowski, Mike 37
Kramer, Tommy 17

INDEX

Robinson, Eugene 34
Robinson, Johnny 34
Robustelli, Andy 54
Rogers, Charlie 50
Rogers, George 13, 14, **61**
Romanowski, Bill 57
Ross, Dan **67**, 69, 75
Rouen, Tom 48
Rypien, Mark 72

Sanders, Barry 10, 11, 12, 13, 14, **15**, 42, 43, 60, 61, 88
Sanders, Deion 35, 36, 37, 52, 88
Sanders, Ricky 65, 67, 69
Sanders, Spec 34
Sandifer, Dan 34, 35, 37
Sapp, Warren 58
Sauer, George 67
Sauerbrun, Todd 48
Sayers, Gale 13, 14, 15, 40, 43, 50, 51, 60
Scarpitto, Bob 48, 49
Schmidt, Joe 54
Schottenheimer, Marty 80, 81
Scott, Jake 68
Seifert, George 80, 81
Sellers, Ron 33
Seno, Frank 51
Shanahan, Mike 81
Sharpe, Shannon 31, 59, 75
Sharpe, Sterling 28, 30
Shaw, Bob 43
Shaw, Pete 53
Shofner, Del 31
Shula, Don 17, **78-79**, 80, 81
Sikahema, Via 52
Simmons, Clyde 39, 57
Simms, Phil 16, 17, 22, 23, 26, 68, **69**
Simpson, Bill 77
Simpson, O.J. 11, 43, 61
Sims, Billy 13, 14, 43, **61**
Sinclair, Michael 58
Sinkwich, Frank 27
Slater, Jackie 56, **57**
Smith, Anthony 38
Smith, Bruce 39, 58, **76**, 77, 88
Smith, Chuck 39
Smith, Emmitt 10, 11, **12**, 13, 14, 15, 32, 40, 41, 42, 43, 58, 59, 60, 64, 65, 66, 76, 88

Smith, Jimmy 28, 29, 31, 32, 59
Smith, J.T. 52
Smith, Lamar 76
Smith, Neil 77
Smith, Noland 51
Smith, Otis 36, 37
Smith, Robert 13
Smith, Rod 29, 67
Smith, Timmy 64, 66, **67**, 76
Smith, Vitamin 50, 51
Snead, Norm 27
Snell, Matt 66
Snow, Jack 33
Stabler, Ken 20, 27, 74, **87**
Stacy, Bill 37
Stallworth, John 65, 67, 69, 85
Starr, Bart 20, 21, 25, 26, 64, 68, **74**
Staubach, Roger **5**, 20, 21, 64, 68, **71**
Steinfort, Fred 45
Stenerud, Jan 40, 44, 46, 47, 57, 69
Stewart, James 13, 43
Stewart, Kordell 23
Stover, Matt 44, 46, 59, 69
Stoyanovich, Pete 45, 47
Strahan, Michael 39, 58, 88, **89**
Strock, Don 74
Stubblefield, Dana 38, 88, 89
Studstill, Pat 31, 32
Suci, Bob 35
Swann, Lynn 64, 65, 67
Sweetan, Karl 31

Taliaferro, George 48
Tarkenton, Fran 16, 18, 22, 24, 26, **27**
Tatum, Jack 55
Taylor, Charley 18
Taylor, Fred 13, 43
Taylor, Hugh 33
Taylor, Jim 13
Taylor, John **5**, 31, **70**
Taylor, Lawrence 39, 88
Taylor, Lionel 28
Teltschik, John 48, 49
Testaverde, Vinny 16, 17, 20, 22, 23, 24, 27, 55
Theismann, Joe 72, 74
Thomas, Anthony 89

Thomas, Derrick 39
Thomas, Emmitt 34
Thomas, Thurman 10, 11, 14, 15, 60, **64**, 65, 66, 74, 75, 76
Thurman, Dennis 77
Tingelhoff, Mick 56, 57
Tittle, Y.A. 17, 18
Todd, Richard 23, 27
Tolbert, Tony 77
Tomlinson, LaDainian 14
Toon, Al 28
Totten, Willie 55
Towler, Dan 13
Townsend, Greg 38, 39
Tripucka, Frank 27
Tuggle, Jessie **55**
Tunnell, Emlen 34, **36**, 37, 52
Turner, Cecil 51
Turner, Jim 40, 44, 46, 47, 69
Tuten, Rick 49

Unitas, Johnny 16, 18, **19**, 25, 27, 55, 67
Upchurch, Rick 52, 53
Urlacher, Brian 89

Van Brocklin, Norm **17**, 21, 25
Van Buren, Steve 50, 51, 76
Van Note, Jeff 56
Vanderjagt, Mike 40, 46, **47**
Vanover, Tamarick 85
Vaughn, Darrick 51
Vermeil, Dick 81, 89
Vinatieri, Adam **1**, 46, **62-63**, 69
Vincent, Troy 58

Wade, Tommy 27
Walker, Doak 40
Walker, Fulton 52
Walker, Herschel 43, 60, 85
Walls, Everson 34
Walsh, Bill 80, 81
Walter, Dave 55
Ware, Andre 55
Warfield, Paul 30, 33
Warner, Curt 14, 43, 61
Warner, Kurt **8-9**, 16, 17, 18, **19**, 20, 22, 23, 58, 64, 67, 68, 74, 88, **BC**

Washington, Dewayne 37
Waterfield, Bob 27
Waters, Charlie 65, 77
Watkins, Tom 50
Watson, Steve 75
Watters, Ricky 15, 59, 60, 65, 66, 69
Weinke, Chris 24
Wells, Warren 33
West, Charlie **53**
Westbrook, Michael 85
White, Danny 20
White, Randy 91
White, Reggie 38, **39**, 77, 88
Wilburn, Barry 68
Wilder, James 14, 61
Wilkins, Jeff 47, 69
Williams, Aeneas 36, **54**, 58, 77
Williams, Bobby 50
Williams, Clarence 13
Williams, Dave 85
Williams, Doug 67, 68, 72, **73**
Williams, John L. 75
Williams, Reggie 54
Williams, Ricky 14, 90
Williams, Travis **50**, 51
Wilson, Jerrel 49
Winslow, Kellen 29, 43, **75**
Woodley, David 67, 74
Woods, Don 14
Woods, Ickey 13, 43
Woodson, Abe 50, 51
Woodson, Charles 89
Woodson, Rod 34, **36**, 37, 51, 58, 88
Wright, Jeff 77
Wright, Louis 85
Wright, Rayfield 65

Yepremian, Garo **84**
Young, Buddy 50, 53
Young, Rickey 29
Young, Steve **7**, 17, 18, 20, **21**, 22, 25, 67, 68, 74, 88

Zendejas, Tony 45, 47
Zorn, Jim 24

CREDITS

PHOTOS

Cover John McDonough
1 Vinatieri: Richard Mackson
2-3 Christiansen: Vernon Biever;
Randle: Tami Tomsic
4-5 Cunningham: Kevin Reece;
Payton: Al Messerschmidt;
Staubach: Fred Kaplan;
Taylor: Bob Rosato;
Lincoln: Charles Aqua Viva;
Marino: Tony Tomsic
6-7 Graham: Frank Rippon;
Young: Bob Rosato
8-9 Warner: Greg Crisp
10-11 Dillon: Marty Morrow;
Brown: Tony Tomsic;
Payton: Al Messerschmidt
12-13 Nevers: Pro Football Hall of
Fame; Smith: Kevin
Terrell/NFLP; Dickerson:
Peter Read Miller
14-15 James: Evan Pinkus;
Anderson: Glenn James;
Sanders: John Reid III
16-17 Fouts: Damian Strohmeyer;
Van Brocklin: Vic Stein;
Marino: Tony Tomsic
18-19 Luckman: Pro Football Hall
of Fame; Warner: Greg
Crisp; Unitas: Tony Tomsic
20-21 Baugh: Pro Football Hall of
Fame; Anderson: Pete Groh;
Young: Bob Rosato
22-23 Moon: Pete Groh;
Favre: Todd Rosenberg;
Montana: Peter Brouillet
24-25 Bledsoe: Mark Brettingen;
O'Donnell: Bill Mount;
Graham: Frank Rippon
26-27 Elway: Todd Rosenberg;
Tarkenton: Vernon Biever;
Cunningham: Kevin Reece
28-29 Rice: Greg Crisp;
Fears: Vic Stein

30-31 Moss: Joe Robbins;
Groman: Lou Witt;
Hutson: NFL Photos
32-33 Largent: Brian Drake;
Irvin: Paul Spinelli/NFLP;
Alworth: NFL Photos
34-35 Krause: Vic Stein; McNeil:
Lou Witt; Lane: NFL Photos
36-37 Tunnell: Frank Rippon;
Woodson: Paul Jasienski;
Houston: Manny Rubio
38-39 Kearse: Allen Kee;
Jones: Malcolm Emmons;
White: Phil Masturzo
40-41 Anderson: Todd Rosenberg;
Andersen: Philip Williams;
Hornung: Tony Tomsic
42-43 Faulk: Kevin Terrell/NFLP;
Moore: NFL Photos
44-45 Mare: Steven Murphy;
Karlis: Michael Minardi;
Dempsey: Otto Greule
46-47 Peterson: George Gojkovich;
Vanderjagt: Allen Kee;
Elam: Allen Kee
48-49 Lary: Frank Rippon;
Gardocki: Christopher
Condon;
Bennett: Peter Brouillet
50-51 Williams: David Boss;
Matson: Russ Reed;
Mitchell: Joe Patronite
52-53 Christiansen: Vernon Biever;
Metcalf: Scott Wachter;
West: Vernon Biever
54-55 Williams: Kevin
Terrell/NFLP; Jackson: Scott
Cunningham;
Tuggle: Greg Crisp
56-57 Blanda: NFL Photos;
Slater: Peter Brouillet;
Marshall: Tony Tomsic
58-59 Randle: Tami Tomsic;
Bettis: Christopher Condon;
Brown: James D. Smith

60-61 Mason: Joe Robbins/NFLP;
Rogers: Michael Yada;
Sims: Andy Hayt
62-63 Vinatieri: Richard Mackson
64-65 Thomas: Bob Rosato;
Lodish: Joe Robbins
66-67 Allen: John Biever;
Ross: Al Messerschmidt;
Smith: Tony Tomsic
68-69 Kelly: Ron Vesely;
Simms: Gin Ellis;
Christie: Herb Weitman
70-71 Taylor: Bob Rosato;
Staubach: Fred Kaplan;
Dyson: Philip Williams
72-73 McConkey: Michael Zagaris;
Aikman: Manny Rubio;
Williams: Michael Zagaris
74-75 Starr: Malcolm Emmons;
Kosar: Mike Moore;
Winslow: Al Messerschmidt
76-77 Smith: George Gojkovich;
Lott: Michael Zagaris;
Lincoln: Charles Aqua Viva
78-79 Shula: Phil Masturzo
80-81 Madden: John Biever;
Landry: Paul Spinelli;
Lombardi: Malcolm
Emmons
82-83 Soldier Field: David
Stluka/NFLP; Rose Bowl:
Manny Rubio
84-85 Yepremian: Richard
Raphael; Quick: Ed Mahan;
Hearst: Greg Trott
86-87 Miami: Dave Cross;
SF: Richard Mackson;
Stabler: A.N. Anderson
88-89 Lewis: Cappy Jackson;
Strahan: Henry Ordosgoitia
90-91 Boston: Greg LeBoeuf;
Hirsch: NFL Photos
Back Cover Warner: Greg Crisp;
Hutson: NFL Photos

SOURCES

A majority of the statistical information was provided by the Elias Sports Bureau. Other lists were compiled by the author from various sources, including *Total Football II* and the *2002 NFL Record & Fact Book*.

ABOUT THE AUTHOR

Matt Marini is an Associate Editor for NFL Creative, based in Los Angeles. He is the editor of the *NFL Record & Fact Book*.